The Rise of China

Books from
FOREIGN AFFAIRS

America and the World: Debating the New Shape of International Politics *(2002)*

The Clash of Civilizations? The Debate (1996)

How Did This Happen? Terrorism and the New War
Edited by James F. Hoge, Jr. and Gideon Rose *(2001) PublicAffairs*

The American Encounter:
The United States and the Making of the Modern World
Edited by James F. Hoge, Jr. and Fareed Zakaria *(1997) BasicBooks*

FOREIGN AFFAIRS
Editors' Choice

Globalization: Challenge and Opportunity *(2002)*

The Middle East in Crisis *(2002)*

The Rise of China *(2002)*

The War on Terror *(2002)*

Closing the Great Divide: Development and the Eradication of Poverty *(2001)*

Intervention and American Foreign Policy *(2001)*

The New Terrorism *(2001)*

The New Trade Agenda *(2001)*

The United States and the Persian Gulf *(2001)*

The United States and Russia *(2001)*

Weapons of Mass Destruction: Threat and Response *(2001)*

Foreign Affairs Agenda: The New Shape of World Politics *(1999)*

Is Global Capitalism Working? *(1999)*

Competitiveness: An International Economics Reader (1994)

For additional information visit
www.foreignaffairs.org/reader/reader.html

FOREIGN AFFAIRS EDITORS' CHOICE

The Rise of China

A Council on Foreign Relations Book

FOREIGN AFFAIRS

NEW YORK

Distributed by
W.W. Norton & Company
500 Fifth Avenue
New York, New York 10110

Founded in 1921, the Council on Foreign Relations is a nonpartisan
membership organization, research center, and publisher. It is dedicated to increasing
America's understanding of the world and contributing ideas to U.S. foreign policy.
The Council accomplishes this mainly by promoting constructive discussions and by publishing
Foreign Affairs, the leading journal on global issues. The Council is host to the widest possible
range of views, but an advocate of none, though its research fellows and Independent Task Forces
do take policy stands. From time to time, books and reports written by members of the Council's
research staff or others are published as a "Council on Foreign Relations Book."

**The Council takes no institutional position on policy issues and has no
affiliation with the U.S. government. All statements of fact and expressions of
opinion contained in all its publications are the sole responsibility of the author or authors.**

The Council's bimonthly magazine, *Foreign Affairs,* has been America's leading publication on
international affairs and foreign policy for 80 years. With a circulation of 115,000 worldwide,
Foreign Affairs has long been the most influential forum for important new ideas, analysis, and
debate on significant global issues. To subscribe, or for more information, visit
www.foreignaffairs.org.

Foreign Affairs books are distributed by W.W. Norton & Company (www.wwnorton.com).

Contents

Introduction

Siddharth Mohandas

ATHENS AND SPARTA?

IN RECENT YEARS Washington and Beijing have had some very public collisions, such as those following the bombing by a U.S. plane of the Chinese embassy in Belgrade in 1999 and the downing of an American spy plane over China in 2001. Yet the relationship has also seen notable instances of cooperation, such as Congress' approval of permanent normal trade relations with China in 2000 and U.S. support for China's admission into the World Trade Organization in 2001. In considering which is more likely in the future, conflict or cooperation, it is worth recalling the observation by Thucydides more than two thousand years ago that what made the Peloponnesian War inevitable was "the growth of Athenian power and the fear which this caused in Sparta." Some today believe that as China's power grows this age-old dynamic is destined to play itself out once again, and that the recent clashes are the harbingers of greater conflicts to come. Others are confident that the game of international relations has changed so much that such fears are groundless. The essays collected here explore the nature and implications of China's rise from a variety of angles, and hopefully, they will help readers form their own opinions.

Originally published in *Foreign Affairs*, the articles fall into four broad categories. The first examines the geopolitical significance of China's rise. The second focuses on Taiwan, the issue with the greatest potential to provoke a major Sino-American conflict. The third explores various other issues that require extended individual treatment, from China's trade relations to its environmental problems

SIDDHARTH MOHANDAS is Associate Editor at *Foreign Affairs*.

to its growing AIDS crisis. And the fourth category, finally, looks at the trajectory of Chinese political development and the challenges its political leaders are facing. Together these essays highlight the most important analytical questions about China today while also suggesting some broad answers.

THE GIANT AWAKES

DISCUSSIONS OF CHINA'S enormous potential have a long history. Napoleon was reputedly a believer, exclaiming, "China? There lies a sleeping giant. Let him sleep! For when he wakes he will move the world." In the past decade, many observers have argued that the giant is beginning to stir. Such appraisals begin with the area in which China is indisputably gigantic: its population of 1.3 billion people. Traditionally, this mass of people has been viewed in the West as potentially the greatest market on earth. In the nineteenth century, British mill owners were convinced that manufacturing shirts for the Chinese would keep them in business for decades; today, American executives eye the China market with equal enthusiasm.

China's current economic resurgence traces back to reforms instituted in 1978 by then paramount leader Deng Xiaoping. Beijing partially dismantled the centrally planned economy and replaced it with a more market-based system. The government no longer collectivized agriculture, allowed managers and entrepreneurs more freedom, and slowly opened up the economy to foreign trade and investment. The economic transformation, coyly called "socialism with Chinese characteristics," was best summed up by Deng's declaration, remarkable for a Communist leader, that "to get rich is glorious."

The results of reform have been dramatic. GDP has quadrupled since 1978. Some of the most explosive growth seems to have come in the past few years: although official Chinese statistics are notoriously unreliable, outside analysts have estimated GDP growth rates of eight to nine percent in recent years and a total GDP in 2000 of $1.1 trillion dollars. If differences in international prices are taken into account, that figure rises to $4.5 trillion—making China the second or third largest economy in the world. Some doubt whether such growth can be sustained, or whether it has even occurred, pointing to the highly uneven development between China's coastal and inland regions and the inaccuracy of Chinese economic data. Nevertheless, the growth figures have convinced many observers that China's moment has arrived, eliciting enthusiasm in some quarters and foreboding in others and forming the backdrop to the discussion in the following pages.

OFFENSE OR DEFENSE?

ONE OF THE MOST URGENT QUESTIONS being asked about China's burgeoning wealth is what it is being spent on. Statistics on Chinese military spending are even more opaque than the national economic data, but all observers agree that defense expenditures have risen throughout the last decade. In 2002, Beijing announced a 17.6 percent increase that would raise the officially declared military budget to $20 billion. Actual spending, however, is widely considered to be several times larger, since significant items such as weapons procurement and research and development costs are excluded from the official version. Analysts therefore believe China has the largest military budget in Asia.

This money has gone to a substantial program of weapons modernization and acquisition for the 2.5-million-strong People's Liberation Army, the largest standing armed force in the world. Recent Chinese purchases from Russia include SU-27 fighter aircraft, S-300 surface-to-air missiles, Kilo-class submarines, and Sovremenny-class destroyers. This shopping spree has sparked concern among China's neighbors, even though the mainland still lags significantly behind its neighbors Japan and Taiwan in the technological sophistication of its military. Beyond its acquisitions, Beijing has also sold nuclear missile technology to nations such as Iran and Pakistan, moves that many view as irresponsible and potentially destabilizing.

Embedded in discussions of China's military programs is a deeper question: What does China want? Is it a status quo power—that is, one willing to function within the existing international order—or is it trying to shake up the international system through force of arms? This question lies at the heart of the first set of essays. Richard Bernstein and Ross Munro assert that China is an aggressive power seeking to become a regional hegemon. The United States, they argue, must therefore energetically act to contain China to protect American power in Asia. Robert Ross disagrees, arguing that China is basically conservative in its foreign policy and thus will remain a status quo power for the foreseeable future. Moreover, Ross says, China is not especially powerful in global terms, which gives the United States the luxury of trying engagement first before resorting to more aggressive actions. Gerald Segal, finally, asks the provocative question, "Does China matter?" He considers the entire debate over how China intends to wield its new power in the international system to be misplaced, because that power has been routinely exaggerated. The country should be treated for what it is, Segal claims—a second-rank middle power like Brazil.

STRAIT TALK

AN IMPORTANT SUBSIDIARY QUESTION to the one about China's potential revisionism is whether Beijing is likely to use force to resolve its territorial disputes. China claims the Spratly and Paracel islands in the South China Sea, both of which are also claimed by Taiwan and Vietnam, and the former by Malaysia and the Philippines as well. Everyone wants a piece of them because all sides suspect that these islands cover significant oil reserves. China's neighbors (and the United States) also worry that Beijing will use the islands as a strategic base to establish hegemony over the South China Sea and the waterway's vital shipping lanes. China has conducted periodic military exercises in the area and there have been occasional armed incidents, most famously when the Chinese occupied Mischief Reef in 1995. Nevertheless, the South China Sea has been termed a "flash point" for more than a decade, and the disputes have so far been handled successfully, or at least put off, through a series of conferences under the aegis of the Association of Southeast Asian Nations. Another volatile dispute, which has also been contained thus far, is over a set of islands in the East China Sea which China calls the Diaoyu and Japan the Senkaku.

China's most dangerous unresolved claim, however, is to the island of Taiwan. The Communists won the Chinese Civil War in 1949 by defeating the Nationalist Kuomintang Party, which subsequently took refuge on Taiwan. For several decades both sides claimed to be the sole legitimate government of China and committed themselves to reunification; in recent years, however, Taiwan has asserted its independence from the mainland. The United States is bound to support Taiwan, both by long-standing historical ties and by treaty (the 1979 Taiwan Relations Act). This commitment—combined with Beijing's firm goal of reunification, by arms if necessary—makes Taiwan the possible spark for a major war between China and the United States.

Trying to finesse this delicate situation, Washington has pursued a policy of "strategic ambiguity" about what it would do in the event of an invasion of Taiwan. The hope is that uncertainty on both sides—with Taiwan being unable to count on U.S. support if it declares independence, and China unable to rule out U.S. intervention if it invades—will induce caution. Indeed, the most significant recent standoff across the Taiwan Strait ended peacefully when, in 1996, China lobbed missiles over the island on the eve of the Taiwanese presidential election, and the United States responded by moving two aircraft carrier groups to the area.

The first of this collection's articles on Taiwan is by the island's former president, Lee Teng-hui. He argues that international perceptions of Taiwan must be brought in line with reality: Taiwan is not a "renegade province," as mainland propaganda would have it, but a thriving democracy and market economy. Kurt Campbell and Derek Mitchell, meanwhile, review recent developments and analyze the likelihood of conflict across the Taiwan Strait. They warn that Washington's strategic ambiguity only adds to the misunderstanding between Beijing and Taipei and may in fact embolden the two potential belligerents. Together the essays paint a picture of rapidly shifting political and strategic environments and the necessity of a nimble and nuanced U.S. response.

GROWING PAINS

BEYOND TAIWAN, there are any number of complex issues that must be understood to add color and depth to the portrait of Chinese modernization. Four are highlighted here. The first relates to the environmental consequences of China's dramatic growth. If each Chinese citizen were to consume as many fossil fuels as an average American, for example, the global environment would quickly be overwhelmed. Elizabeth Economy argues that China's leaders have struck a Faustian bargain in which they have deferred contemplating long-term environmental damage for the short-term benefits of economic growth. This situation must be remedied, she claims, and may even provide a fruitful avenue for U.S. engagement.

Brad Roberts, Robert Manning, and Ronald Montaperto argue that China has unwisely been ignored in U.S. strategizing about nuclear weapons, and in particular in planning for national missile defense. They provide a survey of Chinese nuclear doctrine and deployment that documents Beijing's determined efforts to modernize its modest nuclear force. The authors warn that if NMD does not take into account China's nuclear posture, it might prompt increased Chinese missile deployment and even a Sino-Russian nuclear alliance—thus decreasing American security rather than increasing it.

Bates Gill, Jennifer Chang, and Sarah Palmer, meanwhile, tackle the large and largely unacknowledged problem of HIV/AIDS in China today. They find that the government has not accurately estimated the extent of the crisis and that a flawed health care system provides nowhere near adequate care to most victims. China is on the verge of a major AIDS epidemic, in short, one that could threaten the nation's economic and political stability.

And Joseph Quinlan, finally, looks at the U.S.-China trade deficit, which stood at $80 billion in 2001. Contrary to what trade hawks argue, Quinlan says, this figure does not indicate the failure of American firms to access the Chinese market. He considers economic ties between the two nations to be much deeper than the trade statistics suggest, because the relationship is characterized by extensive U.S. foreign direct investment in China and substantial sales by the affiliates of U.S. companies in the country. If this larger picture is not clearly understood, he worries, it may be difficult to stave off resentments and recriminations within the United States that could trigger a costly trade war.

Introduction

THE LAST BATCH of essays examines the relationship, if one exists, between China's economic and political development. The country's sweeping economic liberalization has not yet been matched by commensurate political liberalization, raising a crucial question: For how long will China's rigid political system be able to withstand the stresses emerging from the country's social and economic transformation?

The growing tensions between state and society were most vividly displayed during the 1989 Tiananmen Square protests, which the Chinese authorities brutally suppressed. The subsequent release of the "Tiananmen Papers" chronicling high-level Communist Party meetings during the crisis revealed a political elite deeply concerned about its legitimacy and hold on power. The stability of the Chinese state now depends on its ability to address the growing grievances of an economically empowered but politically disenfranchised population. As Communist ideology has lost currency, the government must also seek legitimacy elsewhere—whether it turns to economic development or aggressive nationalism will have profound implications for China's foreign policy as well as its domestic situation.

George Gilboy and Eric Heginbotham argue that China's "brittle state" will have to change to meet the new demands placed upon it. They identify significant groups who are growing restive under the current system and argue that China's new leadership will be driven to allow a political transformation allowing greater consultation and openness—so long as a major conflict with the United States does not get in the way.

One of the most difficult internal challenges any reform effort will have to surmount will be ethnic separatism, a problem Chien-peng Chung highlights in his article on the Muslim Uighurs of China's northwest Xinjiang province. Some Uighurs have turned to violence to press their demand for autonomy, he notes, while China has taken advantage of the post–September 11 environment to launch a crackdown under the guise of pursuing its own "war on terror."

And Minxin Pei, finally, examines the challenges that the next generation of Chinese leaders will have to face. He finds that the political reforms of the 1990s have stagnated, the state has been severely weakened by widespread corruption and can barely fulfill its basic functions, such as tax collection, and the Communist party has lost its grassroots organizational capacity. In short, these pieces portray a society in deep flux and a political system struggling to keep up, with the success or failure of the reform effort likely to be the defining story of China's foreseeable future.

QUESTIONS AND ANSWERS

THE ESSAYS ASSEMBLED HERE lay out some of the most important questions about China's rise: Will it become an economic giant? Is it a status quo power? Is it likely to invade Taiwan? Will its development be derailed by AIDS or environmental devastation? Is it democratizing? The authors present their own varied answers, but even when they agree, at this point their assessments can only be provisional. What we can know for sure is that the relationship between China and the United States will be one of the most important of the twenty-first century, with vital implications for both countries as well as the rest of the international system. This volume provides a road map for thinking about that relationship clearly and critically. How to translate such thought into wise policy choices, however, remains perhaps the greatest unanswered question of all.❧

China I

The Coming Conflict
with America

Richard Bernstein and Ross H. Munro

THE RISING ASIAN HEGEMON

FOR A quarter-century—indeed, almost since Richard Nixon signed the Shanghai Communiqué in 1972—a comforting, even heart-warming notion has prevailed among many policymakers and experts on American policy toward the People's Republic of China. They believe that China will inevitably become more like the West—non-ideological, pragmatic, materialistic, and progressively freer in its culture and politics. According to them, China is militarily weak and unthreatening; while Beijing tends toward rhetorical excess, its actual behavior has been far more cautious, aimed at the overriding goals of economic growth and regional stability.

While this vision of China, and especially its diplomatic and economic behavior, was largely true until the middle to late 1980s, it is now obsolete, as it ignores many Chinese statements and actions that suggest the country is emerging as a great power rival of the United States in the Pacific. True, China is more open and

RICHARD BERNSTEIN is a *New York Times* book critic and was *Time* magazine's first Beijing Bureau Chief. ROSS H. MUNRO was Beijing Bureau Chief for the Toronto *Globe and Mail* and is Director of the Asia program at the Foreign Policy Research Institute. This article is drawn from their recent book, *The Coming Conflict With China* by Richard Bernstein and Ross H. Munro, copyright © 1997 by Richard Bernstein and Ross H. Munro. Used by permission of Alfred A. Knopf, a division of Random House, Inc.

internationally engaged than at any time since the communist revolution of 1949. Nevertheless, since the late 1980s Beijing's leaders, especially those who have taken over national policy in the wake of Deng Xiaoping's enfeeblement, have set goals that are contrary to American interests. Driven by nationalist sentiment, a yearning to redeem the humiliations of the past, and the simple urge for international power, China is seeking to replace the United States as the dominant power in Asia.

Since the late 1980s, Beijing has come to see the United States not as a strategic partner but as the chief obstacle to its own strategic ambitions. It has, therefore, worked to reduce American influence in Asia, to prevent Japan and the United States from creating a "contain China" front, to build up a military with force projection capability, and to expand its presence in the South China and East China Seas so that it controls the region's essential sea-lanes. China's sheer size and inherent strength, its conception of itself as a center of global civilization, and its eagerness to redeem centuries of humiliating weakness are propelling it toward Asian hegemony. Its goal is to ensure that no country in the region—whether Japan seeking oil exploration rights in the East China Sea, Taiwan inviting the Dalai Lama for an official visit, or Thailand allowing American naval vessels to dock in its ports—will act without taking China's interests into prime consideration.

TACTICALLY TACTFUL

CHINA AND the United States have, to be sure, been through phases of friendship and tension, with some of the latter unrelated to China's hegemonic goals. At times relations have soured because of inconsistent American policies, especially on human rights and trade matters, that have irritated China's leaders and produced a nationalistic reaction among intellectuals and ordinary Chinese alike. China's current leaders understand the value of stable relations with Washington and under the right terms will accept, as President Jiang Zemin recently did, a resumption of the ceremonies of high-level exchanges.

But China's willingness, even eagerness, to improve the Sino-American mood represents a tactical gesture rather than a strategic one. Since its setback in the Taiwan crisis of early 1996—when China's decision to stage large-scale military exercises in the Straits of Taiwan during Taiwan's presidential election drew harsh criticism from the international community and led the United States to deploy two aircraft carrier task forces to the region—Beijing has tempered its confrontational rhetoric and retreated from some of the actions that most annoyed Washington. China's deference reflects its continued interest in the burgeoning trade and technology transfer relationship with the United States and its hope of quelling anti-Chinese sentiment in Congress and among the American public. When Jiang Zemin comes to Washington in the next year or two, many Americans will likely regard the visit as a sign of a restored sense of common interests. Influential Chinese planners like General Mi Zhenyu, vice-commandant of the Academy of Military Sciences in Beijing, on the other hand, will see it as the next step in bringing China's strength and influence up to par with the United States. "For a relatively long time it will be absolutely necessary that we quietly nurse our sense of vengeance," Mi wrote last year. "We must conceal our abilities and bide our time."[1]

China's goal of achieving paramount status in Asia conflicts with an established American objective: preventing any single country from gaining overwhelming power in Asia. The United States, after all, has been in major wars in Asia three times in the past half-century, always to prevent a single power from gaining ascendancy. It seems almost indisputable that over the next decade or two China will seek to become the dominant power on its side of the Pacific. Actual military conflict between the United States and China, provoked, for example, by a Chinese attempt to seize Taiwan by force or to resolve by military means its territorial claims in the South China Sea, is always possible, particularly as China's military strength continues to grow.

Even without actual war, China and the United States will be adversaries in the major global rivalry of the first decades of the

---

[1]*Megatrends China*, Beijing: Hualing Publishing House, May 1996.

century. Competition between them will force other countries to take sides and will involve all the standard elements of international competition: military strength, economic well-being, influence among other nations and over the values and practices that are accepted as international norms. Moreover, the Chinese-American rivalry of the future could fit into a broader new global arrangement that will increasingly challenge Western, and especially American, global supremacy. China's close military cooperation with the former Soviet Union, particularly its purchase of advanced weapons in the almost unrestricted Russian arms bazaar, its technological and political help to the Islamic countries of Central Asia and North Africa, and its looming dominance in East Asia put it at the center of an informal network of states, many of which have goals and philosophies inimical to those of the United States, and many of which share China's sense of grievance at the long global domination of the West. Samuel Huntington of Harvard University has argued that this emerging world order will be dominated by what he calls the clash of civilizations. We see matters more in the old-fashioned terms of political alliance and the balance of power. Either way, China, rapidly becoming the globe's second most powerful nation, will be a predominant force as the world takes shape in the new millennium. As such, it is bound to be no strategic friend of the United States, but a long-term adversary.

MIGHT LEANS RIGHT

ONE COMMON view of China holds that its integration into the world economy will make it more moderate and cautious in its foreign policy and more open and democratic at home. But the alternative view sees China's more aggressive behavior of the last five years as a consequence of its growing economic and military strength and as linked to its intensifying xenophobic impulses. China's more modern economy and its greater economic influence are already giving it the power to enhance its authoritarianism at home, resist international dissatisfaction with its policies and practices, and expand its power and prestige abroad in ways hostile to American interests.

China's ability to resist and ultimately beat back efforts by the Clinton administration to protest Chinese human rights abuses by withholding most-favored-nation status is a case in point. While complaining bitterly about the American use of economic pressure for political goals, the Chinese applied powerful economic and political pressure on both the United States and elsewhere—notably in Europe and the United Nations—to force President Clinton to retreat from his earlier position. The irony in Sino-American relations is that when China was in the grip of ideological Maoism and displayed such ideological ferocity that Americans believed it to be dangerous and menacing, it was actually a paper tiger, weak and virtually without global influence. Now that China has shed the trappings of Maoism and embarked on a pragmatic course of economic development and global trade, it appears less threatening but is in fact acquiring the wherewithal to back its global ambitions and interests with real power.

Many factors contribute to China's more assertive stance, not least its sense of being Asia's naturally dominant power—an attitude that has not been lost on some regional leaders. As former Singaporean Prime Minister Lee Kuan Yew recently put it, "Many medium and small countries in Asia are uneasy that China may want to resume the imperial status it had in earlier centuries and have misgivings about being treated as vassal states having to send tribute to China as they used to in past centuries." More immediate and concrete shifts in China's strategic attitude can be traced to major events of the late 1980s and early 1990s that increased the power and prestige of China's conservative nationalists and the military, a power shift exacerbated by the incapacitation of paramount leader Deng Xiaoping, who tended to exert a pro-American and moderating influence.

The first of those events was the Tiananmen Square demonstrations of May and June 1989. The rise of a powerful anti-party movement convinced Chinese Communist Party conservatives of the need to maintain stricter control over the country's intellectuals and to "strike hard" (in the current anticrime campaign parlance) against dissenters. Concurrently, the collapse of the Soviet Union removed China's main regional security threat and increased, virtually overnight, China's comparative power in Asia. More important for the conservative-nationalist faction, Mikhail Gorbachev's attempted reform program was taken in Beijing as a powerful negative example, an illustration of the mortal danger to party authority posed by piecemeal liberal political reforms. The third event, the Gulf War, had, as David Shambaugh of George Washington University put it, a "jarring effect" on the People's Liberation Army, whose power and prestige had increased dramatically in the wake of Tiananmen and Deng's enfeeblement. The war demonstrated in the most graphic terms imaginable just how far behind the country was in terms of military technology. "This was the PLA's first exposure to a high-tech war, and they were stunned," Shambaugh has written. Their shock led them to press for a rapid and expensive modernization of China's armed forces, including further nuclear testing and long-range-missile development. The Chinese understood that they would have to master the techniques demonstrated by the Americans if they were to pose a credible threat of their own, whether in the disputed areas of the South China Sea or in any eventual expedition to "liberate" Taiwan.

THE NUMBERS GAME

NOTHING COULD be more important in understanding China's goals and self-image than its military modernization program. China's official position, which is given credence in many Western analyses, is that its primary goal is to develop a world-class economy while maintaining a defensive military force. The official annual defense budget of $8.7 billion—compared to the $265 billion spent annually by the United States or even the $50 billion spent by Japan—seems to support that claim. In reality, almost every major study of Chinese military spending, whether conducted by the U.S. Government Information Office or the International Institute for Strategic Studies, has concluded that actual spending is at least several times Beijing's official figure.

The official budget, for example, does not include the cost of the People's Armed Police, even though it consists mostly of former soldiers demobilized to reduce the size of the army and serves as a reserve available for use in an international conflict. The official budget also excludes nuclear weapons development and soldiers' pensions. When the Chinese purchased 72 SU-27 fighter jets from Russia in 1995 for about $2.8 billion, the entire amount was covered by the State Council and was not deemed a defense expenditure.[2] The official numbers also exclude the cost of research and development. Part of the funding for the development of nuclear weapons, for example, comes from the Ministry of Energy budget, and part of the money for aircraft development comes from the Ministry of Aeronautics and Astronautics Industry. Beijing also excludes proceeds from arms sales, which totaled nearly $8 billion between 1987 and 1991 alone, as well as income from businesses and industries owned and operated by the army, which, with unknown and largely unaccounted-for resources, has quietly become a major player in the global economy.[3]

Realistic analyses of China's defense budget (or those of any other country's, for that matter) must also take into account purchasing power parity—the difference between what something would cost in China and what it would cost elsewhere. As much as 68 percent of Chinese expenditures, from soldiers' salaries and pensions to weapons systems and supplies, which the PLA purchases at artificially low state-set prices, cost a fraction of their equivalent American value. Taking all these factors into account, a conservative estimate of China's actual military expenditures would be at least ten times the officially announced level. In other words, China's real annual defense budget amounts to a minimum of $87 billion per year, roughly one-third that of the United States and 75 percent more than Japan's. Moreover, the figure was 11.3 percent higher in 1996 than in 1995, and 14.6 percent higher in 1995 than in 1994. Even adjusting for inflation, that is still an exceptionally high rate of growth. No

---

[2]June Teufel Dreyer, "Chinese Strategy in Asia and the World," paper prepared for the First Annual Strategy Forum Conference on China, U.S. Naval Academy, Annapolis, Maryland, April 27-28, 1996.

[3]Chong-Pin Lin, "Chinese Military Modernization: Perceptions, Progress, and Prospects," paper given at the American Enterprise Institute Conference on the People's Liberation Army, Staunton Hill, Virginia, June 17-19, 1994, p. 11.

other part of the Chinese government budget has increased at a rate anywhere near that, whether adjusting for inflation or not.

It is true, as the more optimistic analysts point out, that China poses little direct military threat to the United States. But comparing the two countries to highlight Chinese shortcomings is a pointless and misleading exercise, and not only because China's actual military expenditures are a moving target. Whatever the exact figures, China is now engaged in one of the most extensive and rapid military buildups in the world, one that has accelerated in recent months even as China's rhetoric has softened and Beijing has moved to improve its ties with the United States. Driven by its setback in the Taiwan crisis last year and disturbed by the awesome power of the two American aircraft carrier task forces dispatched to the waters near the Straits of Taiwan, China has stepped up its efforts to acquire two capabilities: a credible Taiwan invasion force and the capacity to sink American aircraft carriers should the United States interfere militarily in the China-Taiwan issue.

Even before the Straits of Taiwan incident, China was acquiring airborne early warning technology in Europe and Israel and developing its own in-flight refueling techniques to extend the range of its warplanes. Since the incident, it has sealed a deal with Russia to acquire two destroyers equipped with modern cruise missiles. In the past several years, China has acquired SU-27 fighter-bombers and Russian Kilo-class submarines. In the last three years, China has built 34 modern warships on its own and developed a fleet of M-9 and M-11 mobile-launched missiles of the sort fired near Taiwan during the crisis. It has also expanded its rapid reaction force from 15,000 to 200,000 men and built an airfield in the Paracel Islands and an early warning radar installation on Fiery Cross Reef in the Spratlys. China is the only Asian country to deploy nuclear weapons and the world's third-largest nuclear power in terms of the number of delivery vehicles in service, having surpassed Britain and France by the late 1970s.[4]

As time passes, in other words, it will become far riskier for Washington to preempt Chinese aggression with the kind of over-

---

[4] Ibid., p. 11.

whelming show of force made during the Straits of Taiwan crisis. With the largest army, navy, and air force in Asia, China spends more both relatively and absolutely than any of its neighbors, with the possible exception of Japan, whose modern forces are untested and whose operations could be severely hampered by pacifist leanings at home. In short, China's relative strength gives it the ability to intimidate regional foes and win wars against them. If it continues its rapid military modernization, China will soon become the only country capable of challenging American power in East Asia—and only the United States will have the influence to counterbalance China's regional ascendancy. Moreover, China's goals go a long way toward explaining its tactical attitude toward its relations with the United States, where an annual trade imbalance approaching $40 billion has helped China finance its arms acquisitions. China's mercantilist policies, which include large-scale technology transfers from American sources and the purchase of dual-use technologies in the American market, are likely to become a major source of Sino-American conflict as Beijing grows stronger.

A DEMOCRATIC PEACE?

OF COURSE, if China became a democracy its military build-up would be far less threatening than if it remained a dictatorship. But while the forces pushing toward global democracy are probably too powerful for China to remain unaffected by them forever, there is no reason to believe that China will become democratic in the near future. In the first place, that would be contrary to Chinese political culture. In its entire 3,000-year history, China has developed no concept of limited government, no protections of individual rights, no independence for the judiciary and the media. The country has never operated on any notion of the consent of the governed or the will of the majority. Whether under the emperors or the party general secretaries, China has always been ruled by a self-selected and self-perpetuating clique that operates in secret and treats opposition as treason.

For there to be real democratic reform, the bureaucrats in and near that clique would have to relinquish some of their power, and

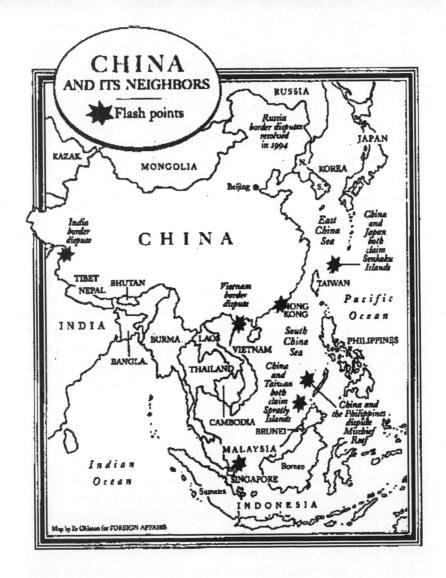

CHINA
AND ITS NEIGHBORS

★ Flash points

Map by Ib Ohlsson for FOREIGN AFFAIRS

there is no sign that they are ready to do so. Receiving personal benefits from political power is a Chinese tradition, whether the benefits involve a state-maintained harem, servants provided by the state, or a Mercedes-Benz donated by a Japanese or overseas Chinese businessman in exchange for an import license. The bureaucracy will not voluntarily relinquish such perks for the sake of democratic principles imported from the West.

Moreover, China's leaders are probably sincere in their equation of democratic reform with social chaos. China has made great strides in creating a more prosperous life for tens of millions of its people, but it remains a potentially unstable nation where the gap between rich and poor is growing, restlessness and unemployment are rampant, and rising expectations have turned the minds of many. The population seems to be at once happy with rising standards of living and discontented with corruption, crime, petty abuses of power by local officials, and the precariousness of life without the guarantees the state once provided. China's leaders, facing the prospect of social uprisings, are sure to stress patriotic solidarity and unquestioned leadership. They cannot be counted on to relinquish their monopolistic hold on power.

Finally, for China's government, subjecting itself to the popular will would mean abdicating its control in areas where it feels the national interest allows no such loss. If, for example, Tibet were to be governed by democratic principles rather than diktat from Beijing, the Tibetan people would create an independence movement that would challenge Chinese control. Similarly, democracy in China would force China's leaders to acknowledge the right of the people of Taiwan to decide the shape of their own future. But granting any such power to the Taiwanese would sabotage China's nonnegotiable insistence on reunification. It would also provide an unwanted precedent for the people of the mainland: if the Taiwanese are consulted on the issue of their political identity, why not the rest of the people of China? China's ruling clique shows no willingness to suffer the loss of power and prestige that a move toward real democracy would entail.

The most likely form for China to assume is a kind of corporatist, militarized, nationalist state, one with some similarity to the fascist states of Mussolini or Francisco Franco. China already has a cult of the state as the highest form of human organization, the entity for whose benefit the individual is expected to sacrifice his or her own interests and welfare. The army is emerging as the single most powerful institution in the country. It has ultimate political authority and has created a large number of influential business enterprises. Unlike the Soviet Union, China is not becoming a powerful military power founded on a pitifully weak economy, but a powerful economy creating a credible military force. It promises to be a state based on the continued rule of a disciplined party that controls information and demands political obedience.

Completing this picture of China is a wounded nationalism, a sense of unredeemed historical suffering, and a powerful suspicion of foreigners. Given the decline of ideology and the passing of the country's charismatic leaders, the government encourages and exploits such sentiments in an effort to enhance its legitimacy and control. When those sentiments prove insufficient to maintain order, the army and the leaders can turn to a vast, intrusive security and police system operating in close cooperation with a compliant judiciary to maintain their undisputed power.

TAIWAN'S DIRE STRAITS

THE GENERAL conditions for Sino-American conflict spring from China's desire to replace the United States as Asia's great power. But there is another, more immediate potential flashpoint: the complex and intractable problem of Taiwan. The Taiwan situation comprises two irreconcilable elements: the people of Taiwan do not want to be ruled by the current Beijing regime, but Beijing has made reunification too important a goal to relinquish. As China grows militarily and the regime runs out of patience, the possibility of an invasion increases. As one Chinese foreign affairs specialist in Beijing told us, "Historically, Chinese leaders have believed in force. Force worked in Tiananmen. It intimidated the intellectuals, and that paved the way for economic growth and political stability. It is realpolitik. And in the Chinese value system, sovereignty, national unification, and preserving the regime have always been higher than peace."

If China invades Taiwan, the United States will be under enormous pressure to prevent a military takeover—or else lose forever its claim to be the great-power guarantor of stability in the Asia-Pacific region. Taiwan thus epitomizes the challenge that China's greater assertiveness and determination to dominate Asia pose for the United States. But there are other places where China's actions and the United States' interests could conflict, the South China Sea being the most obvious. China's buildup of naval, air, and amphibious forces will enable it to seize and hold control of almost the entire South China Sea, now divided between

Vietnam, Malaysia, Brunei, and the Philippines. Indeed, China's stated goal is to occupy islands and outcroppings so far to the south that Chinese forces would almost be in sight of Singapore and Indonesia. That would place China astride the only viable international sealane connecting the Pacific with the Indian Ocean. If China succeeded in extending its control over Taiwan, it would simultaneously gain control of the two southern approaches to Japan, the Taiwan and Luzon Straits. There are signs in articles and statements from Beijing that China increasingly views Taiwan as a strategic prize as well as a renegade province.

Conflict is possible even in areas where China and the United States share interests, as with preventing trouble on the Korean peninsula. When Korea is finally reunified, as it almost surely will be, China will likely press for a withdrawal of American forces from northeast Asia, save for troops in Japan to inhibit remilitarization. As long as Korea remains divided, China will accept the American military presence there to avoid a peninsula-wide war. But once that danger has passed, China will use its influence in northeast Asia for two purposes, both of them inimical to American interests: to bring about a pro-Chinese, anti-American, and anti-Japanese stance in Korea, and to perpetuate Japan's status as a non-normal country, one without the right to assume primary responsibility for its own defense. China could thus assure its predominance in Asia vis-à-vis the only country in the region with the size and strength to challenge it.

THE NEW STRATEGIC TRIANGLE

THE PRIMARY American objective in Asia must be to prevent China's size, power, and ambition from making it a regional hegemon. Achieving that goal requires maintaining the American military presence in Asia and keeping it vastly more powerful and effective than China's armed forces. Furthermore, preventing China from expanding its nuclear weapons arsenal should clearly be an American goal. In the worst-case scenario, Sino-American relations would witness the reappearance of a nuclear standoff reminiscent of the Cold War, with each side relying on the doctrine of mutually assured destruction to prevent an attack from the other. In fact, China has numerous incentives to avoid a nuclear arms race. The United States should play a quiet but effective role in building international pressure to persuade China to make its current moratorium on nuclear weapons testing permanent. Washington should also actively fight against nuclear proliferation in China and elsewhere. The third element in maintaining a balance of power involves Taiwan—specifically, ensuring that it maintains a credible defensive deterrent such that reunification, should it occur, would be voluntary.

The growth of Chinese power has made America's overarching attitude toward Japan obsolete. The United States can no longer operate on the assumption that a weak Japan is a good Japan. If that was once true, it was only because China was poor and weak. In the post-Cold War world, it is Japan's weakness that threatens peace and stability by creating a power vacuum that the United States alone can no longer fill. A strong Japan, in genuine partnership with the United States, is vital to a new balance of power in Asia. A weak Japan benefits only China, which wants no stabilizing balance of power but Chinese hegemony, under which Japan would be little more than Beijing's most useful tributary state.

The difficulties here are considerable. The United States cannot block Chinese hegemony in Asia unless Japan is an equal and willing partner in the process. But if it pushes Japan, the result could well be an anti-American reaction there. Resolving that dilemma might be the single most important task of American diplomacy in the near future. The United States must demonstrate that it is a reliable ally—as it did last spring in the waters near Taiwan—while waiting for Japan to come to grips with an increasingly threatening security environment. China's determination to achieve hegemonic status in Asia will probably facilitate this. But the United States and Japan must realize they need each other.☯

China II

Beijing as a Conservative Power

Robert S. Ross

NEITHER BELLIGERENT NOR BENIGN

RECENT DISCUSSION of Sino-American relations has focused on the development of a U.S. policy for managing a rising power and potential rival. The debate over containment versus engagement is at the center of this discussion. Advocates of containment foresee the rise of a belligerent power, a process that will inevitably destabilize Asia and challenge vital U.S. interests. Arguing that a powerful China will be intent on achieving a long list of unrealized territorial and political ambitions, they insist that the United States must respond to China's rise by strengthening its alliances on the Chinese periphery and increasing U.S. military deployments in Asia. Advocates of engagement agree that China is growing stronger but argue that Chinese intentions remain fluid and that premature adoption of belligerent policies risk creating a self-fulfilling prophecy—treat China as an enemy and it will be one. They assert that expanded economic relations and official dialogues on security issues, human rights, and the global commons will maximize the prospect that China will use its power in a manner conducive to U.S. interests.

ROBERT S. ROSS is Professor of political science at Boston College and a research associate at the John King Fairbank Center for East Asian Research at Harvard University. He is the author, with Andrew J. Nathan, of the forthcoming book, *The Great Wall and the Empty Fortress: China's Search for Security*.

The difference between these two policy packages is significant, but they share a concern for China's increasing ability to destabilize the regional balance of power and threaten vital American interests. In both cases, this concern is based on incorrect assumptions about Chinese strategic capabilities. The reason there is not a "China threat" is not because China is a benign status quo power, but rather because it is too weak to challenge the balance of power in Asia and will remain weak well into the 21st century. Nonetheless, China is not a second-rate power. It has the ability to inflict considerable damage on a wide range of U.S. interests.

The United States needs a policy to contend with China's potential for destabilizing the region, not a policy to deal with a future hegemon. What is most striking about Chinese foreign policy is its effort to consolidate regional trends and promote stability. In its policies toward Russia, North and South Korea, Thailand, Burma, and the countries of Indochina, Central Asia, and South Asia, China has emphasized cooperative measures to consolidate existing relationships rather than forceful measures to promote new patterns of relations. China is a revisionist power, but for the foreseeable future it will seek to maintain the status quo—and so should the United States.

BALANCING ACT

IN THE LATE 1980s, the People's Republic of China emerged as one of the most powerful countries on the East Asian mainland. It had established its strategic authority on the Korean peninsula in the early 1950s, when it held the U.S. military to a standstill and inflicted unacceptable casualties on American soldiers. Since then its capabilities in northeast Asia have grown, giving it a strong voice in peninsular affairs. After the demise of the Soviet Union and the disintegration of the Russian armed forces, China established conventional military control along the full length of its border with Russia and projected a powerful presence throughout the region. What is most striking about this development is that the United States and its allies have accommodated themselves to Chinese power in northeast Asia. Because of a continued U.S. regional presence, America's allies have not considered China's strategic power a threat to the regional balance.

China has also established superiority in Indochina with the acquiescence of the United States. Indeed, the United States welcomed China as a substitute for American power in Indochina throughout the 1970s and 1980s. In an era of declining U.S. capability, the Nixon Doctrine explicitly called for American reliance on regional powers as counterweights to the U.S.S.R. In Indochina and much of Southeast Asia, China was the regional power of choice. Washington was grateful for Beijing's ability to reassure Thailand against the Soviet Union and Vietnam in the wake of its withdrawal from the Vietnam War. Throughout the 1980s Washington supported Chinese efforts to roll back Soviet influence in Southeast Asia by helping the Khmer Rouge to resist the Soviet-sponsored Vietnamese occupation of Cambodia.

In 1989, when the Vietnamese military finally withdrew from Cambodia, Indochina fell within China's strategic sphere of influence. Having ousted the French, the Americans, and the Russians, China no longer confronts a rival in this region. As in northeast Asia, America and its allies accommodated themselves to China's preeminence. Neither the United States nor its traditional partners in Southeast Asia have considered the substitution of Chinese strategic dominance for Soviet power a challenge to their vital security interests.

Chinese strategic authority on mainland East Asia is a long-established characteristic of the region's balance of power. Since the early 1970s, it has not elicited fears of Chinese regional hegemony or calls for China's containment. On the contrary, East Asia's status quo is widely considered an appropriate foundation for a stable regional order. Concern over a Chinese challenge to the regional balance of power—the most vital U.S. interest in East Asia—must focus on the rise of Chinese power beyond the mainland and into the maritime regions of East Asia. Specifically, it must focus on China's ability to become a military power in the East China Sea or the South China Sea.

CHINA AT SEA

CHINA'S AUTHORITY in the East China Sea relies on airpower. Its proximity to the East China Sea allows it to use land-based airpower to influence naval activities in the region. But China's air force remains a primitive war-fighting machine. Its inventory is composed mainly of 1950s- and 1960s-generation aircraft. While China is working to develop modern planes, its most advanced domestically produced fighter, the F8-II, is the equivalent of a late 1960s U.S. warplane. Even this primitive plane has yet to enter fully into operation. Besides American airpower, China must also contend with the Japanese air force, one of the most advanced in the world. Japanese production of the F2 fighter jet will assure it of defensive air superiority over the East China Sea for the foreseeable future. Moreover, Japanese aircraft are armed with air-to-air missiles far more advanced than their Chinese counterparts, and they enjoy the support of advanced AWACS aircraft and other sophisticated defense technologies. Add to this imbalance in air capability Japan's large fleet of advanced surface warships, its vastly superior technological base, and its self-restraint in defense spending as a share of GNP, and it becomes clear not only that China cannot dominate the East China Sea, but that it is not even a player in the naval balance. Recent acquisitions of Soviet SU-27s, a late 1970s fighter jet, fail to alter this reality since China cannot offset Japan's indigenous ability to manufacture 21st century aircraft. Should a Sino-Japanese arms race develop, Japan could easily augment its superiority in regional waters.

Chinese power could also destabilize the South China Sea, which comprises two distinct military theaters. Its northern reaches include the waters east of Vietnam and the Paracel Islands, territory contested by China, Vietnam, and Taiwan. Here, absent outside influence, Chinese military modernization and arms imports can make a difference. Because this part of the South China Sea is within range of Chinese land-based aircraft, improved Chinese capabilities would challenge Vietnam's ability to defend its coastal waters and its claims to the Paracel Islands. But such a development would merely reinforce current trends in Sino-Vietnamese relations, not destabilize the existing order.

The southern reaches of the South China Sea, including Malaysia, Singapore, Indonesia, and the Philippines, comprise another distinct military region, well beyond the reach of China's land-based aircraft. Air support for Chinese ground forces and naval vessels in the distant waters of the South China Sea would require carrier-based air support. Even air refueling of su-27s is insufficient. Air refueling is complex and does not enable aircraft to loiter over distant waters, providing around-the-clock support for troops and surface vessels deployed near potential adversaries. The Chinese navy would lose a battle in this region against Singapore, Malaysia, or Indonesia, all of which possess advanced American or British aircraft. This fact explains the evident willingness and ability of these countries to occupy Chinese-claimed islands in the South China Sea. Indonesia, for example, has used a show of force to warn China from contesting its claim to the economic zone surrounding Natuna Island.

Despite common fears, China's possession of the Spratly Islands would not offset its poor power projection capability. The Spratly Islands are not strategically significant. They are either underwater much of the time or are too small to support the logistical support for naval operations and the deployments required to protect such support from an adversary's aircraft. The military reality of the Spratly Islands is that they are easy to occupy but difficult to hold. Defending them would drain, not enhance, China's power projection capability.

China will need aircraft carriers to become a great power in the distant waters of the South China Sea, capable of challenging America's influence in the maritime countries of Southeast Asia and its access to the region's strategic shipping lanes. It is not clear that China could meet such an enormous challenge. Construction and deployment of an aircraft carrier requires the most modern technology, advanced pilot skills, and astronomical funding. Moscow did not deploy its first true aircraft carrier until after the Cold War. China is far from possessing the power plant, avionics, and metallurgy technologies required to manufacture a plane that can take off and land on an aircraft carrier in any weather. Its pilots have minimal training over blue water and little experience flying without ground control. Its systems engineers cannot manage the logistics of supplying resources to a carrier and its half-dozen support vessels, the equivalent of a small city at sea. The expense of outfitting a carrier group would require China to skew its defense procurement toward naval power or divert significant resources from important civilian infrastructure projects.

Power projection cannot be purchased abroad. Not only would the expense be prohibitive, requiring import of aircraft carriers, appropriate aircraft, and high-technology avionics, but the necessary managerial expertise is not for sale. Moreover, there are limits to what countries will export to China. Obsolete sample carriers from France, for example, may become available, but the hardware for full power projection can only be developed indigenously.

Despite the obstacles and costs, China might still decide to build an aircraft carrier. Experts estimate that if China began today, the vessel would become operational between 2005 and 2010. And that would be only one carrier. The U.S. Navy estimates that keeping one carrier on location at all times requires a fleet of three. China could not build a third carrier until approximately 2020. Due to inferior managerial skills and logistical facilities, China would probably need more than three carriers to keep one on location in the distant regions of the South China Sea. Moreover, these first-generation Chinese carriers would be half the size of an American carrier, deploying aircraft inferior to those currently deployed by the maritime Southeast Asian countries, much less those deployed by the United States on its far larger and more sophisticated vessels.

Finally, even if China does pursue significant military advancements, its rivals will not be standing still. Given its head start and cooperation with Japan and other regional allies, the United States could maintain its current defense posture and the South China Sea would remain an "American lake" well into the 21st century. But the United States continues to modernize all branches of its military. In developing power projection capability, China would risk a U.S.-Japanese arms buildup, leaving itself relatively weaker, while diverting scarce funds from more pressing military objectives, such as securing its coastal waters.

CHINA'S WILD CARD

DESPITE ITS technological and military backwardness, China can still heighten regional instability by threatening U.S. forces, exacerbating local conflicts, and refusing to cooperate with international regimes, thus requiring the United States to commit additional resources to defend its interests.

China is dissatisfied with many aspects of East Asian politics, Taiwan's independence foremost among them. Reunification with Taiwan is a nationalist objective that reflects Beijing's intent to restore China's dynastic borders and conclude the civil war between the Chinese Communist Party and the Chinese Nationalist Party. Taiwan is thus a sensitive issue in succession politics. China's interests in Taiwan also reflect its objective of establishing secure borders. Located less than 100 miles off the Chinese coast, Taiwan truly can serve as an "unsinkable aircraft carrier." As in the 1950s, it can be employed by an adversary to undermine Chinese security. In this respect, its geopolitical significance is similar to Cuba's importance to the United States. Thus, Chinese leaders actively challenge Taiwan's flexible diplomacy and any indication that it can secure international support for a formal declaration of independence. They are intent on minimizing Taipei's foreign policy independence and ultimately establishing mainland control over Taiwan. As Chinese military maneuvers in March 1996 revealed, they are prepared to worsen regional tensions to promote this objective.

Taiwan is only the most prominent of China's territorial objectives. Beijing rejects Japan's territorial claim to the Diaoyu (Senkaku) Islands, Vietnam's claim to the Paracel Islands, and the claims by Vietnam, Malaysia, the Philippines, and Brunei to the Spratly Islands. It also has a territorial dispute with Vietnam over the demarcation of the Gulf of Tonkin. There is considerable potential for exploiting natural resources, including oil, particularly in the disputed waters in the northern sector of the South China Sea. China insists that it is the rightful claimant to these territories and that its neighbors are taking advantage of its military weakness to infringe on Chinese sovereignty. Territorial ambitions, domestic political instability, and desire for recognition as a regional power encourage Chinese leaders to resist these perceived challenges.

China is a constant threat to engage in weapons proliferation. As a regional power, it has minimal national interest in stability in the Middle East and northern Africa. Hence, it has little incentive for arms control or to forgo profits from weapons or technology exports. Should Chinese leaders decide to maximize profits, disregard U.S. threats of sanctions, and provide missiles to Syria or unsupervised dual-use nuclear technologies to Iran, they could foster regional arms races and embroil the United States in regional conflicts. A resumption of Chinese nuclear testing would undermine America's effort to ban nuclear tests entirely. China could also destabilize the international liberal trade order. Should it develop a mercantilist economic policy or fail to reform its trading system, China could damage global trade more than Japan at the height of its global economic power.

Beijing can use military power to destabilize Taiwan and regional politics. China had a similar ability in the 1950s, when its shelling of the offshore islands caused a crisis in Sino-American relations. Similarly, Chinese missiles can threaten U.S. naval vessels. But this capability is shared by the most primitive militaries, including those of Iran and Argentina. As Iraq showed during the 1991 Persian Gulf War, even a 1960s Scud missile can disrupt local economies and menace U.S. forces. Indeed, the gravest danger posed by China's 1996 missile tests was their obsolescence: the missiles were so primitive that they could have veered off course and hit Taiwan. America must be concerned by Chinese military power not because China will develop hegemonic power but because it can raise the cost of defending American interests and spoil the prospects for a cooperative regional order.

CHINA'S CONSERVATIVE FOREIGN POLICY

CHINA'S ABILITY to wreak havoc is not new to East Asia. Since 1949 the United States has had to cope with U.S.-Chinese conflicts of interest. In many respects, it is easier to deal with these conflicts today than ever before. Indochina is no longer an issue. China is collaborating with South Korea to encourage North Korean moderation. Even the conflict with Taiwan has become more manageable. Taiwan now has a stable government, a prosperous economy, and a vastly improved military. The mainland's ability to challenge Taiwan's security is less today than ever before. Moreover, the mainland is no longer allied with a global superpower that can shield it in a conflict with the United States over Taiwan. Nor is it an antagonist in a polarized East Asian balance of power. Participation in the global economy and a stake in regional stability encourage China to avoid confrontations with the United States over Taiwan.

Despite cooperative relations with almost all of its neighbors in Asia, Chinese foreign relations have not been perfectly harmonious. But the friction does not reflect Beijing's restlessness. It is true that China's Taiwan policy contains significant coercive elements and that Beijing has not relinquished its right to use force against the island. But China's intent is to deter Taipei and Washington from changing the status quo, not to compel Taiwan to expedite the pace of formal reunification. Beijing has made clear that it is prepared to return to the rules that governed U.S.-Taiwan-mainland relations prior to 1994, when Washington did not allow Taiwan's senior officials to visit the United States but supplied it with large quantities of advanced weapons. The friction in Sino-American relations since June 1989 has stemmed primarily from bilateral trade relations, U.S.-Taiwan relations, and American criticism of China's human rights record. Moreover, China has acquiesced to U.S. pressure regarding weapons proliferation. With the exception of its security relationship with Pakistan, since the end of the Cold War Beijing has not exported any missiles in violation of international agreements, nor has it exported technology for use in nuclear reactors not under the International Atomic Energy Agency's supervision.

China's relationship with Japan has become more difficult, but this primarily reflects changes in Japanese politics. Japan's development of a competitive multiparty electoral system has politicized its policy toward Taiwan and Sino-Japanese territorial disputes and promoted linkage between Japanese aid and China's human rights record. Japan has also become a more confident country, less willing to abide

Chinese demands that it maintain a low international profile as penance for its military expansionism in the 1930s and 1940s. During the 1996 dispute over the Diaoyu (Senkaku) islands, China adopted a cautious policy, waiting for Japanese policy to change after the November general elections.

The striking exception to this conservative trend is the Spratly Islands. Since the mid-1970s, China has been trying to diminish the impact of the South China Sea territorial disputes on its relations with the countries in the Association of Southeast Asian Nations. Since the early 1990s, it has advocated cooperative economic ventures in the disputed waters and shelving of the sovereignty disputes. But in early 1995 Beijing expanded its control of territory also claimed by the Philippines, arousing heightened concern throughout the region. This action remains an anomaly in China's relations with the ASEAN countries. It is too early to say whether this incident reflects a new trend in Chinese policy or a brief digression designed to deter widespread land seizures in Southeast Asia.

Since the early 1980s, the world's major industrial economies have been eager to participate in Chinese modernization. The prospect of China's economic growth and greater domestic employment has encouraged them to expand trade and investment ties with China. They have also been willing to extend considerable foreign aid and technical assistance through bilateral and multilateral institutions. The accompanying technology and capital transfers have played an important role in modernizing Chinese industry and stimulating economic growth. Beijing realizes that conservative international behavior was the precondition that encouraged the advanced industrial countries to participate in China's economy. They also realize that provocative policies risk ending China's economic success story.

A stable regional order is conducive to Chinese ambitions insofar it allows Beijing to focus its domestic resources on the economic foundations of strategic power. The growth of the Chinese military budget since the late 1980s has been significant, if only because it has allowed China to import advanced Russian weaponry. Recent increases in the military budget partially reflect high inflation affecting soldiers' salaries and the cost of consumer goods purchased by the Chinese military. Nonetheless, estimates of the overall size of

China's military budget indicate that China's defense spending remains relatively low, both as a share of gross national product and compared with the spending of other great powers.

THE LUXURY TO ENGAGE

THUS FAR, post-Cold War international relations have not hardened into opposing blocs. The opportunity still exists to establish a stable international order. But the sine qua non of such an order is Chinese participation in its creation. Chinese leaders remain committed to seeking constructive relations with all their neighbors. Given the costs that China can impose on America and its allies, U.S. policy should take advantage of that posture to reinforce China's interest in regional stability and strengthen its commitment to global stability. Engagement, not isolation, is the appropriate policy.

Engagement must mean more than simply offering China the opportunity to follow the rules. It requires acknowledging Chinese interests and negotiating solutions that accommodate both American and Chinese objectives. In bilateral relations, this will entail compromise approaches over the future of Taiwan. It will require mutual accommodation to prevent nuclear proliferation on the Korean peninsula and accommodation of Chinese interests in Sino-Pakistani security ties. Washington must acknowledge the economic sources of trade imbalances and the Chinese government's limited ability to enforce its domestic laws and international commitments.

Engagement also requires multilateral collaboration with Chinese interests. The United States and the other major powers must invite China to participate in international rule-making. This includes encouraging Chinese membership as well as leadership responsibilities in various arms control regimes, including the Missile Technology Control Regime, the Zangger Committee, and the Nuclear Suppliers Group, which regulate nuclear-related exports, the Australia Group on chemical precursors and biological agents, and the Wassenaar Arrangement, the successor to the Coordinating Committee on Multilateral Export Controls, which tracks trade in conventional weapons and technologies. It also entails admitting China into the World Trade Organization on terms that reflect both U.S. concern for China's significant influence in the international economic system and the less-developed conditions of China's domestic economy.

Engagement will not be easy. For it to succeed, China must be willing to accommodate important U.S. interests in controlling proliferation of all kinds of weapons, whether or not proscribed by international regimes, in regions where the United States has vital interests, including the Middle East. China will have to make a formal commitment to reform its economic system and sustained efforts to enforce its international economic commitments. It will also have to make allowances for American domestic conditions and political values, especially as they affect U.S. economic policy and human rights diplomacy. Finally, China will have to use its leadership responsibilities wisely, seeking to consolidate a broadly beneficial international society, rather than striving for unilateral gains at the expense of international stability.

There is no guarantee that engagement will work. It will often involve acrimonious negotiations as the two sides make difficult policy adjustments and seek compromise solutions. At times, Washington will have to protect its interests unilaterally. It will also have to maintain its current military deployments in Asia. U.S. strategic retrenchment would do far more to alter the Sino-American bilateral balance of power and the regional balance of power than any combination of Chinese military and economic policies. But it is also clear that reliance on purely coercive measures will not elicit Chinese cooperation. Rather, it would almost guarantee renewed tension in Sino-American relations and heightened instability in East Asia. Given the strategic head start the United States and its allies enjoy, Washington has the luxury of observing Chinese modernization before adopting a more assertive posture.☯

Does China Matter?

Gerald Segal

MIDDLE KINGDOM, MIDDLE POWER

DOES CHINA MATTER? No, it is not a silly question—merely one that is not asked often enough. Odd as it may seem, the country that is home to a fifth of humankind is overrated as a market, a power, and a source of ideas. At best, China is a second-rank middle power that has mastered the art of diplomatic theater: it has us willingly suspending our disbelief in its strength. In fact, China is better understood as a theoretical power—a country that has promised to deliver for much of the last 150 years but has consistently disappointed. After 50 years of Mao's revolution and 20 years of reform, it is time to leave the theater and see China for what it is. Only when we finally understand how little China matters will we be able to craft a sensible policy toward it.

DOES CHINA MATTER ECONOMICALLY?

CHINA, UNLIKE Russia or the Soviet Union before it, is supposed to matter because it is already an economic powerhouse. Or is it that China is on the verge of becoming an economic powerhouse, and you must be in the engine room helping the Chinese to enjoy the benefits to come? Whatever the spin, you know the argument: China is a huge market, and you cannot afford to miss it (although few say the same about India). The recently voiced "Kodak version" of this argument is that if only each Chinese will buy one full roll

GERALD SEGAL was Director of Studies at the International Institute for Strategic Studies in London and co-author, with Barry Buzan, of *Anticipating the Future*.

of film instead of the average half-roll that each currently buys, the West will be rich. Of course, nineteenth-century Manchester mill owners said much the same about their cotton, and in the early 1980s Japanese multinationals said much the same about their television sets. The Kodak version is just as hollow. In truth, China is a small market that matters relatively little to the world, especially outside Asia.

If this judgment seems harsh, let us begin with some harsh realities about the size and growth of the Chinese economy. In 1800 China accounted for 33 percent of world manufacturing output; by way of comparison, Europe as a whole was 28 percent, and the United States was 0.8 percent. By 1900 China was down to 6.2 percent (Europe was 62 percent, and the United States was 23.6 percent). In 1997 China accounted for 3.5 percent of world GNP (in 1997 constant dollars, the United States was 25.6 percent). China ranked seventh in the world, ahead of Brazil and behind Italy. Its per capita GDP ranking was 81st, just ahead of Georgia and behind Papua New Guinea. Taking the most favorable of the now-dubious purchasing-power-parity calculations, in 1997 China accounted for 11.8 percent of world GNP, and its per capita ranking was 65th, ahead of Jamaica and behind Latvia. Using the U.N. Human Development Index, China is 107th, bracketed by Albania and Namibia—not an impressive story.

Yes, you may say, but China has had a hard 200 years and is now rising swiftly. China has undoubtedly done better in the past generation than it did in the previous ten, but let's still keep matters in perspective—especially about Chinese growth rates. China claimed that its average annual industrial growth between 1951 and 1980 was 12.5 percent. Japan's comparable figure was 11.5 percent. One can reach one's own judgment about whose figures turned out to be more accurate.

Few economists trust modern Chinese economic data; even Chinese Prime Minister Zhu Rongji distrusts it. The Asian Development Bank routinely deducts some two percent from China's official GDP figures, including notional current GDP growth rates of eight percent. Some two or three percent of what might be a more accurate GDP growth rate of six percent is useless goods produced to rust in warehouses. About one percent of China's growth in 1998 was due to massive government spending on infra-structure. Some three percent of GDP is accounted for by the one-time gain that occurs when one takes peasants off the land and brings them to cities, where productivity is higher. Taking all these qualifications into account, China's economy is effectively in recession. Even Zhu calls the situation grim.

China's ability to recover is hampered by problems that the current leadership understands well but finds just too scary to tackle serious-ly—at least so long as East Asia's economy is weak. By conservative estimates, at least a quarter of Chinese loans are nonperforming—a rate that Southeast Asians would have found frightening before the crash. Some 45 percent of state industries are losing money, but bank lending was up 25 percent in 1998—in part, to bail out the liv-ing dead. China has a high savings rate (40 percent of GDP), but ordinary Chinese would be alarmed to learn that their money is clearly being wasted.

Some put their hope in economic decentralization, but this has already gone so far that the center cannot reform increasingly waste-ful and corrupt practices in the regions and in specific institutions. Central investment—20 percent of total investment in China—is falling. Interprovincial trade as a percentage of total provincial trade is also down, having dropped a staggering 18 percent between 1985 and 1992. Despite some positive changes during the past 20 years of reform, China's economy has clearly run into huge structural impediments. Even if double-digit growth rates ever really existed, they are hard to imagine in the near future.

In terms of international trade and investment, the story is much the same: Beijing is a seriously overrated power. China made up a mere 3 percent of total world trade in 1997, about the same as South Korea and less than the Netherlands. China now accounts for only 11 percent of total Asian trade. Despite the hype about the impor-tance of the China market, exports to China are tiny. Only 1.8 per-cent of U.S. exports go to China (this could, generously, be perhaps 2.4 percent if re-exports through Hong Kong were counted)—about the same level as U.S. exports to Australia or Belgium and about a third less than U.S. exports to Taiwan. The same is true of major

European traders. China accounts for 0.5 percent of U.K. exports, about the same level as exports to Sri Lanka and less than those to Malaysia. China takes 1.1 percent of French and German exports, which is the highest in Asia apart from Japan but about par with exports to Portugal.

China matters a bit more to other Asian countries. Some 3.2 percent of Singapore's exports go to China, less than to Taiwan but on par with South Korea. China accounts for 4.6 percent of Australian exports, about the same as to Singapore. Japan sends only 5.1 percent of its exports to China, about a quarter less than to Taiwan. Only South Korea sends China an impressive share of its exports—some 9.9 percent, nudging ahead of exports to Japan.

Foreign direct investment (FDI) is even harder to measure than trade but sheds more light on long-term trends. China's massive FDI boom, especially in the past decade, is often trumpeted as evidence of how much China does and will matter for the global economy. But the reality is far less clear. Even in 1997, China's peak year for FDI, some 80 percent of the $45 billion inflow came from ethnic Chinese, mostly in East Asia. This was also a year of record capital flight from China—by some reckonings, an outflow of $35 billion. Much so-called investment from East Asia makes a round-trip from China via some place like Hong Kong and then comes back in as FDI to attract tax concessions.

Even a more trusting view of official FDI figures suggests that China does not much matter. FDI into China is about 10 percent of global FDI, with 60 percent of all FDI transfers taking place among developed countries. Given that less than 20 percent of FDI into China comes from non-ethnic Chinese, it is no surprise that U.S. or European Union investment in China averages out to something less than their investment in a major Latin American country such as Brazil. China has never accounted for more than 10 percent of U.S. FDI outflows—usually much less. In recent years China has taken around 5 percent of major EU countries' FDI outflow—and these are the glory years for FDI in China. The Chinese economy is clearly contracting, and FDI into China is dropping with it. In 1998 the United Nations reported that FDI into China may be cut in half, and figures for 1998–99 suggest that this was not too gloomy a guess. Japanese FDI into China has been halved from its peak in 1995. Ericsson, a multinational telecommunications firm, says that China accounts for 13 percent of its global sales but will not claim that it is making any profits there. Similar experiences by Japanese technology firms a decade ago led to today's rapid disinvestment from China. Some insist that FDI flows demonstrate just how much China matters and will matter for the global economy, but the true picture is far more modest. China remains a classic case of hope over experience, reminiscent of de Gaulle's famous comment about Brazil: It has great potential, and always will.

It does not take a statistical genius to see the sharp reality: China is at best a minor (as opposed to inconsequential) part of the global economy. It has merely managed to project and sustain an image of far greater importance. This theatrical power was displayed with great brio during Asia's recent economic crisis. China received lavish praise from the West, especially the United States, for not devaluing its currency as it did in 1995. Japan, by contrast, was held responsible for the crisis. Of course, Tokyo's failure to reform since 1990 helped cause the meltdown, but this is testimony to how much Tokyo matters and how little Beijing does. China's total financial aid to the crisis-stricken economies was less than 10 percent of Japan's contribution.

The Asian crisis and the exaggerated fears that it would bring the economies of the Atlantic world to their knees help explain the overblown view of China's importance. In fact, the debacle demonstrated just how little impact Asia, except for Japan, has on the global economy. China—a small part of a much less important part of the global system than is widely believed—was never going to matter terribly much to the developed world. Exaggerating China is part of exaggerating Asia. As a result of the crisis, the West has learned the lesson for the region as a whole, but it has not yet learned it about China.

DOES CHINA MATTER MILITARILY?

CHINA IS a second-rate military power—not first-rate, because it is far from capable of taking on America, but not as third-rate as most of its Asian neighbors. China accounts for only 4.5 percent of global defense spending (the United States makes up 33.9 percent) and 25.8 percent of defense spending in East Asia and Australasia. China poses a formidable threat to the likes of the Philippines and can take islands such as Mischief Reef in the South China Sea at will. But sell the Philippines a couple of cruise missiles and the much-discussed Chinese threat will be easily erased. China is in no military shape to take the disputed Senkaku Islands from Japan, which is decently armed. Beijing clearly is a serious menace to Taiwan, but even Taiwanese defense planners do not believe China can successfully invade. The Chinese missile threat to Taiwan is much exaggerated, especially considering the very limited success of the far more massive and modern NATO missile strikes on Serbia. If the Taiwanese have as much will to resist as did the Serbs, China will not be able to easily cow Taiwan.

Thus China matters militarily to a certain extent simply because it is not a status quo power, but it does not matter so much that it cannot be constrained. Much the same pattern is evident in the challenge China poses to U.S. security. It certainly matters that

China is the only country whose nuclear weapons target the United States. It matters, as the recent Cox report on Chinese espionage plainly shows, that China steals U.S. secrets about missile guidance and modern nuclear warheads. It also matters that Chinese military exercises simulate attacks on U.S. troops in South Korea and Japan. But the fact that a country can directly threaten the United States is not normally taken as a reason to be anything except robust in defending U.S. interests. It is certainly not a reason to pretend that China is a strategic partner of the United States.

The extent to which China matters militarily is evident in the discussions about deploying U.S. theater missile defenses (TMD) in the western Pacific and creating a U.S. national missile defense shield (NMD). Theoretically, the adversary is North Korea. In practice, the Pentagon fears that the U.S. ability to defend South Korea, Japan, and even Taiwan depends in the long term on the ability to defend the United States' home territory and U.S. troops abroad from Chinese missiles. Given the $10 billion price tag for NMD and the so-far unknowable costs of TMD, defense planners clearly think that China matters.

But before strategic paranoia sets in, the West should note that the Chinese challenge is nothing like the Soviet one. China is less like the Soviet Union in the 1950s than like Iraq in the 1990s: a regional threat to Western interests, not a global ideological rival. Such regional threats can be constrained. China, like Iraq, does not matter so much that the United States needs to suspend its normal strategies for dealing with unfriendly powers. Threats can be deterred, and unwanted action can be constrained by a country that claims to be the sole superpower and to dominate the revolution in military affairs.

A similarly moderated sense of how much China matters can be applied to the question of Chinese arms transfers. China accounted for 2.2 percent of arms deliveries in 1997, ahead of Germany but behind Israel (the United States had 45 percent of the market, and the United Kingdom had 18 percent). The $1 billion or so worth of arms that Beijing exports annually is not buying vast influence, though in certain markets Beijing does have real heft. Pakistan is easily the most important recipient of Chinese arms, helping precipitate a nuclear arms race with India. Major deals with Sudan, Sri Lanka, and Burma have had far less strategic impact. On the other hand, arms transfers to Iran have been worrying; as with Pakistan, U.S. threats of sanctions give China rather good leverage. China's ability to make mischief therefore matters somewhat—primarily because it reveals that Chinese influence is fundamentally based on its ability to oppose or thwart Western interests. France and Britain each sell far more arms than China, but they are by and large not creating strategic problems for the West.

Hence, it is ludicrous to claim, as Western and especially American officials constantly do, that China matters because the West needs it as a strategic partner. The discourse of "strategic partnership" really means that China is an adversary that could become a serious nuisance. Still, many in the Clinton administration and elsewhere do not want to call a spade a spade and admit that China is a strategic foe. Perhaps they think that stressing the potential for partnership may eventually, in best Disney style, help make dreams come true.

On no single significant strategic issue are China and the West on the same side. In most cases, including Kosovo, China's opposition does not matter. True, the U.N. Security Council could not be used to build a powerful coalition against Serbia, but as in most cases, the real obstacle was Russia, not China. Beijing almost always plays second fiddle to Moscow or even Paris in obstructing Western interests in the Security Council. (The exceptions to this rule always concern cases where countries such as Haiti or Macedonia have developed relations with Taiwan.) After all, the Russian prime minister turned his plane to the United States around when he heard of the imminent NATO attack on Serbia, but the Chinese premier turned up in Washington as scheduled two weeks later.

NATO's accidental May bombing of the Chinese embassy elicited a clear demonstration of China's theatrical power. Beijing threatened to block any peace efforts in the United Nations (not that any were pending), but all it wanted was to shame the West into concessions on World Trade Organization membership, human rights, or arms control. China grandiosely threatened to rewrite the Security Council resolution that eventually gave NATO an indefinite mandate to keep the peace in Kosovo, but in the end it meekly abstained. So much for China taking a global perspective as one of the five permanent members of the Security Council. Beijing's temper tantrum merely highlighted the fact that, unlike the other veto-bearing Security Council members, it was not a power in Europe.

In the field of arms control, the pattern is the same. China does not block major arms control accords, but it makes sure to be among the last to sign on and tries to milk every diplomatic advantage from having to be dragged to the finish line. China's reluctance to sign the Nuclear Nonproliferation Treaty (NPT), for instance, was outdone in its theatricality only by the palaver in getting China to join the Comprehensive Test Ban Treaty. China's participation in the Association of Southeast Asian Nations Regional Forum—Asia's premier, albeit limited, security structure—is less a commitment to surrender some sovereignty to an international arrangement than a way to ensure that nothing is done to limit China's ability to pursue its own national security objectives. China matters in arms control mainly because it effectively blocks accords until doing so ends up damaging China's international reputation.

Only on the Korean Peninsula do China's capacities seriously affect U.S. policy. One often hears that China matters because it is so helpful in dealing with North Korea. This is flatly wrong. Only once this decade did Beijing join with Washington and pressure Pyongyang—in bringing the rogue into compliance with its NPT obligations in the early phases of the 1994 North Korean crisis. On every other occasion, China has either done nothing to help America or actively helped North Korea resist U.S. pressure—most notoriously later in the 1994 crisis, when the United States was seeking support for sanctions and other coercive action against North Korea. Thus the pattern is the same. China matters in the same way any middle-power adversary matters: it is a problem to be circumvented or moved. But China does not matter because it is a potential strategic partner for the West. In that sense, China is more like Russia than either cares to admit.

Gerald Segal

DOES CHINA MATTER POLITICALLY?

THE EASIEST category to assess—although the one with the fewest statistics—is how much China matters in international political terms. To be fair to the Chinese, their recent struggle to define who they are and what they stand for is merely the latest stage of at least 150 years of soul-searching. Ever since the coming of Western power demonstrated that China's ancient civilization was not up to the challenges of modernity, China has struggled to understand its place in the wider world. The past century in particular has been riddled with deep Chinese resistance to the essential logic of international interdependence. It has also been marked by failed attempts to produce a China strong enough to resist the Western-dominated international system—consider the Boxer movement, the Kuomintang, or the Chinese Communist Party (CCP). Fifty years after the Chinese communist revolution, the party that gave the Chinese people the Great Leap Forward (and 30 million dead of famine) and the Cultural Revolution (and perhaps another million dead as well as a generation destroyed) is devoid of ideological power and authority. In the absence of any other political ideals, religions and cults such as the Falun Gong (target of a government crackdown this summer) will continue to flourish.

China's latest attempt to strengthen itself has been the past 20 years of economic reforms, stimulated by other East Asians' success in transforming their place in the world. But the discourse on prosperity that elicited praise for the order-sustaining "Asian values" or Confucian fundamentals was burned in the bonfire of certainties that was the Asian economic crisis. China was left in another phase of shock and self-doubt; hence, economic reforms stalled.

Under these circumstances, China is in no position to matter much as a source of international political power. Bizarre as old-style Maoism was, at least it was a beacon for many in the developing world. China now is a beacon to no one—and, indeed, an ally to no one. No other supposedly great power is as bereft of friends. This is not just because China, once prominent on the map of aid suppliers, has become the largest recipient of international aid. Rather, China is alone because it abhors the very notion of genuine international interdependence. No country relishes having to surrender sovereignty and power to the Western-dominated global system, but China is particularly wedded to the belief that it is big enough to merely learn what it must from the outside world and still retain control of its destiny. So China's neighbors understand the need to get on with China but have no illusions that China feels the same way.

China does not even matter in terms of global culture. Compare the cultural (not economic) role that India plays for ethnic Indians around the world to the pull exerted by China on ethnic Chinese, and one sees just how closed China remains. Of course, India's cultural ties with the Atlantic world have always been greater than China's, and India's wildly heterogeneous society has always been more accessible to the West. But measured in terms of films, literature, or the arts in general, Taiwan, Hong Kong, and even Singapore are more important global influences than a China still under the authoritarian grip of a ruling Leninist party. Chinese cities fighting over who should get the next Asian Disneyland, Chinese cultural commissars squabbling over how many American films can be shown in Chinese cinemas, and ccp bosses setting wildly fluctuating Internet-access policies are all evidence of just how mightily China is struggling to manage the power of Western culture.

In fact, the human-rights question best illustrates the extent to which China is a political pariah. Chinese authorities correctly note that life for the average citizen has become much more free in the past generation. But as Zhu admitted on his recent trip to the United States, China's treatment of dissenters remains inhuman and indecent.

Still, China deserves credit for having stepped back on some issues. That China did not demand the right to intervene to help Indonesia's ethnic Chinese during the 1998–99 unrest was correctly applauded as a sign of maturity. But it was also a sign of how little international leadership China could claim. With a human-rights record that made Indonesia seem a paragon of virtue, China was in no position to seize the moral high ground.

Measuring global political power is difficult, but China's influence and authority are clearly puny—not merely compared to the dominant

West, but also compared to Japan before the economic crisis. Among the reasons for China's weakness is its continuing ambiguity about how to manage the consequences of modernity and interdependence. China's great past and the resultant hubris make up much of the problem. A China that believes the world naturally owes it recognition as a great power—even when it so patently is not—is not really ready to achieve greatness.

DOES IT MATTER IF CHINA DOESN'T MATTER?

THE MIDDLE KINGDOM, then, is merely a middle power. It is not that China does not matter at all, but that it matters far less than it and most of the West think. China matters about as much as Brazil for the global economy. It is a medium-rank military power, and it exerts no political pull at all. China matters most for the West because it can make mischief, either by threatening its neighbors or assisting anti-Western forces further afield. Although these are problems, they will be more manageable if the West retains some sense of proportion about China's importance. If you believe that China is a major player in the global economy and a near-peer competitor of America's, you might be reluctant to constrain its undesired activities. You might also indulge in the "pander complex"—the tendency to bend over backward to accommodate every Chinese definition of what insults the Chinese people's feelings. But if you believe that China is not much different from any middle power, you will be more willing to treat it normally.

This notion of approaching China as a normal, medium power is one way to avoid the sterile debates about the virtues of engaging or containing China. Of course, one must engage a middle power, but one should also not be shy about constraining its unwanted actions. Such a strategy of "constrainment" would lead to a new and very different Western approach to China. One would expect robust deterrence of threats to Taiwan, but not pusillanimous efforts to ease Chinese concerns about TMD. One would expect a tough negotiating stand on the terms of China's WTO entry, but not Western concessions merely because China made limited progress toward international transparency standards or made us feel guilty about bombing its embassy in Belgrade. One would expect Western leaders to tell Chinese leaders that their authoritarianism puts them on the wrong side of history, but one would not expect Western countries to stop trying to censure human rights abuses in the United Nations or to fall over themselves to compete for the right to lose money in the China market.

To some extent, we are stuck with a degree of exaggeration of China's influence. It has a permanent U.N. Security Council seat even though it matters about as much as the United Kingdom and France, who hold their seats only because of their pre–World War II power. Unlike London and Paris, however, Beijing contributes little to international society via peacekeeping or funding for international bodies. China still has a hold on the imagination of CEOs, as it has for 150 years—all the more remarkable after the past 20 years, in which Western companies were bamboozled into believing that staying for the long haul meant eventually making money in China. Pentagon planners, a pessimistic breed if ever there was one, might be forgiven for believing that China could eventually become a peer competitor of the United States, even though the military gap, especially in high-technology arms, is, if anything, actually growing wider.

Nevertheless, until China is cut down to size in Western imaginations and treated more like a Brazil or an India, the West stands little chance of sustaining a coherent and long-term policy toward it. Until we stop suspending our disbelief and recognize the theatrical power of China, we will continue to constrain ourselves from pursuing our own interests and fail to constrain China's excesses. And perhaps most important, until we treat China as a normal middle power, we will make it harder for the Chinese people to understand their own failings and limitations and get on with the serious reforms that need to come.๏

Understanding Taiwan

Bridging the Perception Gap

Lee Teng-hui

THE SUSTAINED ECONOMIC growth, unprecedented prosperity, and full democracy recently achieved by the Republic of China has one drawback: the speed of Taiwan's progress has outstripped prevailing perceptions of what Taiwan is and how it should fit into the global order. To illustrate this, one need look no further than the attainment of full democracy on Taiwan, and the subsequent emergence of a new sense of national identity impelled by the force of the ballot box.

To convey a sense of the popular will on Taiwan today, I now refer to my fellow citizens as "New Taiwanese," meaning those who are willing to fight for the prosperity and survival of their country, regardless of when they or their forebears arrived on Taiwan and regardless of their provincial heritage or native language. This fresh national identity based on the New Taiwanese consciousness, holding that Taiwan's interests should be foremost and that the people of Taiwan all share a common destiny, has gradually harmonized the populace and provided a stable middle ground for Taiwan's political development.

This new sense of identity manifests itself in every aspect of Taiwanese social and political life, including the role that the voters of Taiwan feel is appropriate for their democracy in the world. In turn, the way that its democratic achievements are perceived elsewhere in the region—particularly across the Taiwan Strait in Beijing—directly affects Taiwan's security and future development in ways never anticipated by the international community. If peace and stability are to

---

LEE TENG-HUI is the former President of the Republic of China

be maintained in the Taiwan Strait area, the perceptions underpinning policies involving Taipei and Beijing must be more firmly grounded in reality than in ideological wishful thinking. Only then can the international community faithfully take into account the full significance of democracy on Taiwan.

IMAGINED COMMUNITY

THE PEOPLE of Taiwan have long endured diplomatic isolation, which essentially began with the withdrawal of the Republic of China (R.O.C.) from the United Nations on October 25, 1971. Under pressure from Beijing, many countries were forced to switch official recognition from Taipei to Beijing. The R.O.C. was gradually excluded from most international governmental organizations and maintained formal diplomatic relations with only 29 countries.

After I became president in January 1988, the R.O.C. began to seek a role in the United Nations and other world bodies while stressing that it had no intention of challenging Beijing's status in these organizations. But to this day the authorities in Beijing continue to use every opportunity to isolate my country diplomatically in hopes of turning fiction into reality. It is fiction to claim that the Chinese nation is not divided—and pernicious fiction to assert that the People's Republic of China (P.R.C.) has any right or imperative to claim sovereignty over Taiwan. The attacks that Beijing makes on the legitimacy of the democratic government affront the people of Taiwan and the prevailing values of the international community. Such attacks also threaten world peace and stability.

This is where international perceptions of Taiwan play a crucial role. If the 21st century is to be one not where might makes right but where the rule of law and healthy economic competition provide the basis of lasting world peace, the development of democracy and respect for the right of representation must play a crucial role.

Beijing would have the world fear potential disaster should the people of Taiwan enjoy their inherent right to actual and legitimate representation in international organizations and activities. Day in and day out, the international media duly parrot Beijing's mantra that it "regards Taiwan as a renegade province," as if this were somehow a plausible pretext for the P.R.C. to undermine regional peace and stability in the name of reckless nationalism. Shrill threats from Beijing directed at the "Taiwan authorities," warning that military force would follow a declaration of independence, are faithfully reported as "news."

The only problem with this scenario is that it is not true. The Chinese nation was divided in 1949 when the P.R.C. was proclaimed. Taiwan cannot cause national disintegration, because the Chinese nation is already divided. There is no need to warn against Taiwan's declaring independence because the R.O.C. has been sovereign and independent since its founding in 1912. It does not need to declare independence from the P.R.C., which is a much younger state that exercises effective jurisdiction over a totally different part of the Chinese nation.

STRAW MEN, IRON FISTS

BEIJING has, in effect, set up a straw man by claiming to regard Taiwan as a "renegade province"—over which it has never exercised effective jurisdiction and to which it has no legal claim under international law—so that it has something with which to threaten action whenever the government and people of the R.O.C. seek to exercise their right to representation in the international community. This unstable ideological house of cards is a threat to regional peace and stability.

One vivid example dates from June 16, 1995, when Beijing used my visit to my American alma mater, Cornell University, as a pretext for unilaterally suspending the promising series of talks between the Strait Exchange Foundation (SEF) and the Association for Relations Across the Taiwan Strait (ARATS). Beijing proceeded to "test fire" M-9 missiles in the waters off Taiwan on the eve of Taiwan's presidential election in 1996 to intimidate voters.

Thereafter, the R.O.C. government made more than 100 approaches to the mainland authorities, urging them to resume the SEF-ARATS talks as soon as possible. These overtures were ignored until February 1998, when the mainland leadership finally agreed to resume cross-strait communications. Koo Chen-fu, the chair of SEF, led a delegation to the Chinese mainland in October 1998 and met with Jiang Zemin and other Chinese communist leaders to discuss the future development of cross-strait relations. This visit has put cross-strait relations back on track and paved the way for a resumption of the series of SEF-ARATS consultations.

Nevertheless, these talks cannot be held under the unequal terms on which Beijing has been insisting. Preserving Beijing's tactical straw-man myth of Taiwan as a "renegade province" flies in the face of reality. The R.O.C. has remained a sovereign state since 1912, although its jurisdiction now extends solely to the territories of Taiwan, the Pescadores, Quemoy, and Ma-tsu. Nevertheless, it is the world's 19th-largest economy and its 15th-largest trading country. In the 50 years since the P.R.C. was founded, both sides of the Taiwan Strait have been separately ruled, with neither subordinate to the other. This situation has not changed in any substantive way since 1949.

In 1991, the R.O.C. government demonstrated its goodwill by renouncing the use of force to reunify China, acknowledging Beijing's rule on the Chinese mainland, and seeking to replace military confrontation with peaceful exchanges and dialogue. Despite these initiatives, Beijing continues to belittle Taipei as merely a local government. It has also sought to downgrade the status of the R.O.C. government in cross-strait exchanges and to insist on a hegemonistic interpretation of the "one-China principle" to force Taipei to gradually acquiesce to a "one country, two systems" formula. Simultaneously, Beijing has done its utmost to isolate the R.O.C. diplomatically. Consequently, the international community has become accustomed to Beijing's pronouncements while disregarding the obvious fact that each side of the strait is separately and equally ruled.

The facts have been distorted by Beijing and overlooked by the international community for many years. Cross-strait ties now form a "special state-to-state relationship."

Should the R.O.C. government conduct negotiations with the Chinese communists while claiming that we are only a vague "political entity," we would place ourselves in an unequal position that fails to accord with reality. Thus, before commencing any negotiations, Taipei must clearly define cross-strait relations. To engage in meaningful dialogue with the other side and protect the dignity of our country and the interests of its people, the R.O.C. government must reach out to the other side on the basis of reality. When any two states conduct a dialogue, they do so on an equal basis regardless of size or military prowess. There is no reason for the cross-strait dialogue to be any different. Only talks conducted on an equal basis can win popular support.

BRIDGING THE STRAIT

CROSS-STRAIT relations are inherently special because Taiwan and the Chinese mainland share the same culture, historical origins, and ethnic bonds. The people on the two sides engage in myriad social, economic, and other exchanges, a level of interaction not found in any other divided nation.

What is most important is that the two sides are willing to work in concert and consult on an equal basis to pursue the future reunification of China. If the two sides can recognize and appreciate this special relationship, they can transcend political differences and jointly develop a relationship conducive to the peaceful and democratic reunification of the Chinese nation one day.

But several obstacles must be overcome if cross-strait relations are to flourish in the years ahead. First, mutual trust between Taipei and Beijing has not yet been established. Although people-to-people exchanges have expanded since the ban on visits to the Chinese mainland was lifted in 1987, relations between Taiwan and the mainland are still overshadowed by more than four decades of hostility. People in Taiwan remain highly suspicious of the Chinese communists. Opinion polls conducted over the past few years indicate that most Taiwanese believe that the authorities in Beijing are hostile to them and the R.O.C. government.

Second, the mainland authorities' refusal to renounce the use of force as a means to solve the Taiwan Strait issue presents a large, insurmountable obstacle to improving relations. Beijing's hegemonic attitude has intensified the Taiwanese people's negative impression of the mainland authorities and their repugnance for the lack of political accountability inherent in the mainland Communist Party dictatorship. Every time the authorities in Beijing have tried to intimidate Taiwan with military force, the percentage of Taiwanese voters advocating independence has increased. Thus, contrary to some inaccurate observations voiced overseas, it is not any of Taipei's actions, but rather Beijing's clumsy attempts at intimidation by belligerent rhetoric and provocative saber-rattling that have intensified the call in Taiwan for declaring independence.

Sadly, Beijing's truculent attitude toward Taiwan and its political accomplishments displays a poor understanding of both Taiwan and the nature of diplomacy. No democratically elected government would enter into negotiations without the consent of its people—especially negotiations that might ultimately affect its domestic political accountability.

Third, five decades of separate rule have caused vast differences between the political, social, and economic systems of the two sides of the Taiwan Strait. Taiwan is already a full-fledged democracy; the Chinese mainland remains under authoritarian rule. Taiwan has long been a market economy; the Chinese mainland is mostly a planned economy closely controlled by the state. The mainland authorities disingenuously argue that reunification has nothing to do with the differences in socioeconomic and political systems between the two sides. In fact, the authoritarian nature of the communist regime is the key factor alienating the people of Taiwan from the Chinese mainland.

It is not in anyone's interest to aggravate cross-strait tensions or see the mainland erupt in chaos. The R.O.C. government has no intention whatsoever of provoking Beijing. Its military strategy is defensive in nature, as are its military forces. This government long ago renounced the idea of force as a means of solving cross-strait disputes and is willing to take a pragmatic approach toward improving relations with Beijing. As a leading investor on the Chinese mainland and a major trading partner with the area, the R.O.C. would like to see the mainland remain stable and its people continue to work toward more prosperous lives. Taipei and Beijing can cooperate to maintain peace in the Taiwan Strait and promote the welfare of all Chinese. Therefore, during the past few years Taipei has made numerous concrete proposals: providing the Chinese mainland with the know-how to fight floods, assisting agricultural improvements on the Chinese mainland, exchanging ideas about reorganizing state-owned enterprises, and cooperating to find ways of coping with the after-effects of the

Asian financial crisis. These proposals are aimed at creating a win-win situation for both sides of the Taiwan Strait.

Taipei does not rule out discussing political issues once meetings with Beijing resume on a basis of parity. But priority should be given to outstanding issues that affect people's everyday lives.

Democratic development in Taiwan has now reached the point of no return. The people of Taiwan would never countenance any less-representative form of government. They are glad to see their country willing and able to serve as a responsible member of the international community. For example, the R.O.C. has pledged an aid package equivalent to $300 million to help the Kosovar refugees. The package will provide emergency support for food, shelters, medical care, and education for Kosovars still living in exile in neighboring countries. It will also cover the cost of short-term accommodations for some refugees in Taiwan, with job training to help them restore their homeland upon their return.

Of course, democracy on Taiwan is hardly perfect. No democratic system is. Having achieved full democracy in only one decade, the R.O.C. is still in the process of deepening and consolidating its system. Traditional social values have been discarded while new ones have yet to take hold. Taiwan is engaging in educational and spiritual reform to improve the quality of life by promoting cultural development, teaching new virtues and values while rediscovering traditional ones, and developing the sense of civic and social responsibility.

Only nations willing to relinquish the known certainties of old-style authoritarianism for the unknowns of modern democracy can ultimately enjoy the flexibility, efficiency, and transparency necessary to meet the competitive challenges of globalization sweeping the world today. What Taiwan has done in the past decade is remarkable for the speed and scope of its economic and political changes and for the peaceful way in which such changes have been achieved. It is in the best interest of regional and even global peace and stability for Beijing to embrace democracy rather than try to contain it. The international community has a crucial role to play here—first by updating its perceptions of what has taken place on Taiwan and the implications of democratic development here for the region and the world, and then by working to accord Taiwan the international status and role it deserves.⊛

Crisis in the Taiwan Strait?

Kurt M. Campbell and Derek J. Mitchell

TROUBLE ISLAND

THE APRIL standoff on Hainan Island following the collision of a U.S. spy plane with a Chinese fighter jet was a striking reminder of how troubled the relationship remains between the world's most powerful country and its most populous one. The sources of contention in that standoff—the purpose of reconnaissance flights, the interpretation of national sovereignty, and the handling of public diplomacy—could provoke a future standoff on another, more critical island: Taiwan. Although the spy-plane drama ended happily with the homecoming of the detained American crew, unresolved military and diplomatic issues promise greater discord to come in the U.S.-China relationship—a simmering conflict that could soon explode over the status of Taiwan.

Washington's official relationship with Beijing on the one hand and its unofficial relationship with Taipei on the other represent perhaps the most complex foreign-policy balancing act in the world today. At stake are a number of core U.S. foreign policy goals: the promotion of democracy, the preservation of U.S. credibility, loyalty to traditional allies and friends, the engagement and integration of an emerging power into the international system, and the maintenance of peace and stability in Asia as a whole. The

KURT M. CAMPBELL is Senior Vice President, Director, International Security Program, and Henry A. Kissinger Chair in National Security at the Center for Strategic and International Studies and Deputy Director of the Aspen Strategy Group. DEREK J. MITCHELL is Senior Fellow for Asia at CSIS.

interplay and clash among these various goals make the Taiwan Strait an unpredictable and therefore dangerous place. Moreover, Taiwan's recent democratization has undermined the "one-China" policy and made the prospect of conflict increasingly likely. Compounding the problem is the deep division within the U.S. foreign policy elite over how to maintain the increasingly fragile peace there. Perhaps nowhere else on the globe is the situation so seemingly intractable and the prospect of a major war involving the United States so real.

ONE CHINA, ONE TAIWAN

WHEN MAO ZEDONG and Chiang Kai-shek ruled the mainland and Taiwan, respectively, the issue at stake was not whether there was only one China, but who its legitimate ruler was. Chiang sought to retake the mainland for the Republic of China (ROC), while the People's Republic of China (PRC) sought (and continues to seek) to bring the "renegade province" of Taiwan back into the fold, thus completing the Chinese communist revolution.

The one-China concept, however, has become increasingly blurred in recent years. The PRC has modernized its economy, but its political system remains very similar to the one Mao created more than 50 years ago. Over the same period, Taiwan has developed from an authoritarian state with a primitive economy into a prosperous free-market democracy. Although many observers in the PRC and some in the United States may still view the dispute over Taiwan's status as the last manifestation of a decades-old civil war, developments on the island over the past decade have changed the essential character of the divide.

In 1991, Taiwanese President Lee Teng-hui officially recognized the ROC's lack of authority on the mainland—stating the obvious while effectively severing the lingering political bond between Taipei and Beijing. Then, last year, the Taiwanese people elected President Chen Shui-bian, who has advocated formal independence and whose party has had no ties and little contact with the mainland. Since taking power, Chen's government has questioned the PRC's 1992 declaration of a "consensus" on the one-China principle and has rejected Beijing's requirement that Taipei accept the principle as a prerequisite for dialogue, preferring instead to put the principle itself up for discussion.

After 50 years of de facto independence (not to mention a previous 50 years of Japanese colonialism), Taiwanese citizens have developed a cultural identity distinct from that of their mainland counterparts. The island's mainstream culture is becoming more and more Taiwanese, with the Taiwanese dialect gaining currency over the official Mandarin Chinese dialect, and with Taiwan's indigenous history increasingly being taught in schools. As time passes, the political, cultural, and emotional divide between Taiwan and the mainland will only widen further, even as economic and commercial ties continue to develop.

So far, however, the PRC seems unable to understand and deal effectively with Taiwan's changing political climate. The rise of Chen's Democratic Progressive Party has challenged the mainland's Chinese Communist Party to consider a new paradigm for its relations with the island, but the CCP has yet to implement one. Instead, it continues to develop its ties with the formerly ruling Kuomintang Party through public and private meetings in Beijing and Hong Kong. The PRC's determination to deal with only those Taiwanese who agree with its interpretation of the one-China policy has exacerbated the cross-strait divide.

Moreover, the PRC does not seem to understand that threats more often repel than compel democracies—and that Taiwan is no exception. Instead of offering incentives for Taipei to consider reconciliation, Beijing continues to practice intimidation tactics, including the rapid deployment of missiles across the strait. This coercive policy has proven counterproductive, reducing rather than enhancing the confidence and trust needed for dialogue.

At the same time, Taiwan's transition to democracy has changed the way it manages domestic issues and popular opinion. In the past, the ROC's authoritarian regime could ruthlessly impose its decisions on its people without regard to their will. Today, public attitudes and sentiments play a significant role in shaping government initiatives. Such democratic accountability may moderate the zeal of pro-independence leaders such as Chen, since any elected official must maintain cross-strait stability to stay in office. At the same time, however, democratic account- ability will also prevent any dramatic moves toward the PRC, given the Taiwanese people's preference for the status quo.

Fundamentally, the CCP sees Taiwan's democratic developments as an implicit challenge to its own authority and legitimacy. Last year's ROC presidential election, which led to the first peaceful demo- cratic transition of power in Chinese history (on the mainland or in Taiwan), undercut the CCP's long-standing contention that democra- cy is not consistent with Chinese, or Asian, values. Thus the longer Taiwanese democracy continues to thrive, the more the CCP fears it may serve as a model for disgruntled segments of its own populace.

Moreover, the defeat of the Kuomintang in last year's ROC election represents a passing of the old guard in Taiwan, implicitly challenging the legitimacy of the old guard within the CCP as well. Indeed, the recently published *Tiananmen Papers*, detailing the regime's delibera- tions during the 1989 student uprising in Beijing, portrays a party elite deeply concerned about its political legitimacy and control.

DANGEROUS WATERS

OVER THE LAST 50 YEARS, the Taiwan Strait has been the site of an almost ritualistic pattern of military conflict. The ROC-controlled islands of Quemoy and Matsu, for example, were the scene of a tense Cold War standoff during the 1950s; beginning later that decade and continuing for two more decades, the PRC regularly shelled these islands according to an announced schedule.

After a brief thaw in relations during the 1980s and early 1990s, the Taiwan Strait has been remilitarized over the past five years. The origin of this military escalation is a matter of continuing dispute. Beijing argues the process began in 1992 with the U.S. sale of F-16 fighter aircraft to Taiwan. The Taiwanese counter that they bought the F-16s only in reaction to the PRC's acquisition of a squadron of SU-27 fighter aircraft from Russia. Whatever its origin, this "action-reaction" cycle has led both sides to intensify their military preparations.

The PRC has dusted off war plans previously left on the shelf. Over the last several years, the training regimen, doctrine, writings, weapons procurement, and rhetoric of the People's Liberation Army have all turned to focus on a Taiwan attack scenario. An entire generation of PLA officers has been trained to plan and execute a military invasion of the island. Top generals have been acquiring military support from Russia and Israel to create armaments designed specifically to combat Taiwan (and potential U.S. intervention on the island's behalf), including sophisticated aircraft, missiles, destroyers, and other advanced military technologies. The military systems that Beijing has fielded over the past five years look less like heavily armored bargaining chips and more like true military capabilities that could be used on the battlefield.

In response, Taiwan has started to modify its military institutions, capabilities, and strategies to combat a growing threat from the mainland. The ROC military, for instance, has sought to instill greater professionalism in its ranks and adopt more modern modes of warfare. Taiwan has traditionally taken a purely defensive approach to a potential military conflict with the PRC. But today's strategists suggest that claiming an advantage at an early stage in a clash may be essential for the island's survival, leading ROC military officials to think more in terms of quick strikes and rapid escalation.

Taiwan has also purchased a wide array of advanced defensive weapons, largely from the United States, which is currently its only reliable provider of military assistance. In the past, the ROC had focused on acquiring weapons to counter the growing numbers of ballistic missiles being deployed across the strait by the PRC. This year Taiwan's wish list concentrated on naval weaponry intended to combat any threat of a blockade by the mainland. During the annual arms-sales negotiations this April, Washington agreed to sell Taipei a robust package of naval systems, including diesel submarines, Kidd-class destroyers, P-3C antisubmarine aircraft, advanced torpedoes, and minesweeping helicopters.

Taiwan had also sought to purchase advanced Arleigh Burke–class destroyers equipped with AEGIS air-defense radar—a request that took on deep symbolic meaning for both sides of the strait. Beijing viewed the AEGIS system not only as a potential element of a future missile defense, but also as a harbinger of greater U.S.-Taiwan defense cooperation, which could embolden independence advocates on the island.

At the same time, Taipei viewed the AEGIS technology not only as a necessary defense against a growing air threat from the PRC, but also as a comforting signal that the United States would maintain its commitment to the island's defense. In April, President George W. Bush deferred the AEGIS decision, partly to avoid a dramatic rift in U.S.-China relations so early in his administration. This deferral does not end the controversy, however; it merely postpones it until his administration is more firmly in place. In fact, Bush's decision later that month to end the annual arms-sales negotiation process suggests that he could change his position on the AEGIS issue at any time.

The AEGIS controversy is just one example of how discussions among Washington, Beijing, and Taipei have shifted toward military issues and away from the more promising commercial and economic ones long favored by moderates in all three capitals. During the April arms-sales talks, both sides of the strait placed disproportionate weight on a particular arms sale (the AEGIS system), thus framing the dispute in military rather than political terms. Such a mindset allows both sides to ignore the political issues involved and may unleash a destructive dynamic of military action and reaction.

Exacerbating the problem is the lack of military and political communication between Beijing and Taipei. The assumptions that animate policies in both capitals are often drawn from misleading and contradictory information about the other side. The potential for miscalculation resulting from a lack of understanding and direct contact has grown substantially in recent years. Last year, for example, fighter aircraft from both sides flew perilously close to one another around the arbitrary line that separates the operational training areas of the two armed forces. On several instances, the military aircraft were loaded with live ordnance. As cross-strait flights and military exercises increase, misunderstandings and miscalculations that could escalate into real military conflict will also increase. In today's militarized Taiwan Strait, inadvertence is as dangerous as premeditation.

In an attempt to remedy this situation, the United States has tried over the last several years (albeit mostly at the semi-official level) to encourage both sides to contemplate a host of measures aimed at building trust and improving communication. A number of

Cold War models have been suggested, including a hot line, exercise notification, and a joint air-traffic-control center. These suggestions, coming mostly from the American academic community, have been met with stony silence, particularly from the PRC. After all, the Chinese goal is to erode confidence and security in Taiwan, not enhance it. For its part, the ROC has traditionally rejected confidence-building arrangements for fear that the United States might step back from its defense commitments as a result. Although Taiwan has demonstrated more interest in such measures in recent years, it is unclear whether that interest is genuine or whether it is just a way to distinguish the ROC position from the mainland one.

Not only do the PRC and Taiwan lack military communication, but they also lack political dialogue. Normally such a situation would invite outside mediation to help break the stalemate. However, no such international efforts are underway, either in the United Nations or in Asia's security talk shop, the Association of Southeast Asian Nations' Regional Forum. Although Asian leaders recognize that a cross-strait conflict would be detrimental to regional peace, stability, and development, no one wants to get involved for fear of angering the PRC. Even those Asian leaders who could counsel restraint and mount regional pressure on Beijing have remained silent.

Likewise, the United States has avoided stepping in, despite its important diplomatic role in virtually every other hot spot around the world. Even though the Taiwan Strait is one of the few places in the world where U.S. forces may be drawn into a major conflict at a moment's notice, Washington has refrained from actively helping to ease tensions or to facilitate a resolution of the dispute. This state of affairs strikes many in the security community as particularly curious, if not dangerous.

CROUCHING TIGER, HIDDEN DRAGON

U.S. POLICY toward the Taiwan Strait has often been described as one of "strategic ambiguity." At first, the policy was a primarily political stance: Washington maintained an agnostic position on the ultimate status of Taiwan, requiring only that the matter be settled peacefully, by mutual agreement, and without coercion.

Over time, however, the policy became increasingly defined in military terms. Washington did not make clear what actions it would take in the event of a cross-strait conflict, adhering only to the well-worn verse in the Taiwan Relations Act that the United States would "consider any effort to determine the future of Taiwan by other than peaceful means ... a threat to the peace and security of the Western Pacific area and of grave concern to the United States." Washington refrained from being more explicit about its response, believing that uncertainty would deter both Beijing and Taipei from making any provocative moves.

This policy of ambiguity has become difficult to explain and perhaps even more difficult to implement in recent years. It has hindered routine consultations with U.S. allies because even senior U.S. officials are not sure what Washington would do in the case of a true crisis. It has also severely constrained communication and planning with Taiwan's political and military authorities—essential elements of effective crisis management. In 1995–96, for example, Pentagon planners and intelligence specialists did not know how Taiwan would respond to the PRC's provocative missile tests across the strait. This blind spot in a tense situation was a wake-up call to the United States, leading to a substantial increase in military contact with Taiwan during the Clinton years. These meetings, however, remained unofficial and behind the scenes.

In response to these difficulties, a growing debate has emerged about whether the United States should move toward a policy of more explicit deterrence to prevent both provocative ROC political actions and coercive PRC military steps. Many observers fear that the U.S. policy of strategic ambiguity has been profoundly misinterpreted by both sides: Taiwan believes that in the end, the United States would support its independence, whereas the PRC believes that the United States would stand aside if the bullets ever started to fly. Misapprehensions of this sort can make ambiguity an ultimately dangerous strategy.

During the 2000 presidential campaign, Bush criticized the policy of strategic ambiguity for this very reason. Four months after he took office as president, he told an interviewer on *Good Morning, America* that the United States would do "whatever it takes" to defend Taiwan in the event of a Chinese attack. At first, this statement seemed to counter long-standing policy and provide new clarity to U.S. commitments. But the manner in which Bush made the announcement seemed to reinforce rather than reduce ambiguity concerning U.S. commitments to Taiwan. His statement was not coordinated with Congress or U.S. allies. And in an interview later that day, he reiterated his administration's adherence to the one-China policy—a statement later affirmed by members of his foreign policy team. Whereas Bush's statement appears to have sown concern and some confusion in Beijing, Taipei has warmly embraced the increased clarity, stating that the comment made the U.S. commitment to stability in the region "more convincing."

As demonstrated by Bush's statement, the ambiguity of U.S. policy toward the Taiwan Strait is not entirely strategic. Significant disagreements within Washington muddle the U.S. position and mitigate the policy's effectiveness. This political ambiguity is not new: beginning in the 1950s, conservative Republican legislators used the U.S. commitment to Taiwan—and the related issue of "who lost China"—to attack President Harry Truman for his insufficient anticommunist zeal. And in 1979, Congress passed the Taiwan Relations Act to affirm abiding U.S. security commitments to the island in response to President Jimmy Carter's recognition of the PRC.

This tension between Congress and the White House continues today. Although a general consensus supports both engagement of the PRC and commitment to the security of Taiwan, Washington is becoming increasingly divided into two camps: those who see China as the next major market for the United States, and those who see China as the next major threat to the United States. These concepts are not necessarily mutually exclusive, but they form the basis for lasting tensions within the China-watching community.

More ominously, the sort of bitter ideological—and often personal—conflict seen among Soviet specialists during the Cold War is beginning to emerge within the China-focused community both inside and outside of government. This trend emerged during the sharply partisan later years of the Clinton administration and continues today, marked by periodic news leaks and personal attacks on individual China specialists and policymakers. The continuation of this trend will be chilling to the kind of open, honest, and informed discussion necessary for formulating an effective

China policy. It may ultimately prove dangerous for managing a situation as sensitive as that of the Taiwan Strait.

FINAL ANSWER?

WHEREAS Mao and Deng Xiaoping were willing to wait 50 to 100 years for Taiwan's integration, today's PRC regime expresses a growing sense of impatience. In light of Taiwan's recent political changes, the CCP increasingly believes that time is not on its side—that Taiwan is moving further from the mainland with each passing year. Over the last few years, reports have surfaced about a possible PRC timeline for resolving its dispute with Taiwan. Beijing's February 2000 "white paper," for example, characterized the situation in the Taiwan Strait as "complicated and grim," suggesting a growing pessimistic sentiment that war is inevitable.

More ominously, the paper also enunciated a new reason for using force to resolve the Taiwan issue: the island's indefinite refusal to negotiate reunification. This statement suggested a fundamental change in Beijing's policy toward Taiwan. In the past, the PRC threatened violence should Taiwan depart from the status quo. The 2000 white paper, however, suggests that the PRC would now consider using force should Taiwan cling to the present system.

During the April spy-plane incident, moreover, certain elements of Chinese society, including the youth and the urban intelligentsia, demonstrated growing feelings of nationalism and resentment toward the United States, fueled by state propaganda. Such popular sentiments could drive the CCP to take a harsher approach toward Taiwan and the United States. Should this nationalism grow virulent, or should an economic downturn shake the government's legitimacy, the regime could be compelled to take drastic action toward Taiwan to save itself.

At the same time, Taiwan has displayed increasing impatience with its current lack of international status. As a major player in global trade and investment and as a burgeoning democracy, Taiwan desires a commensurate role in world affairs and an enhanced international profile. This desire will likely increase, clashing with the PRC's strategy of isolating the island.

Crisis in the Taiwan Strait?

The current situation in the Taiwan Strait—the escalating tensions, the lack of meaningful dialogue, and the increasingly hostile rhetoric—suggests that the U.S. approach to the region requires a wholesale review. In the end, Mao's oft-quoted warning about the need for patience in addressing the issue of Taiwan is perhaps more relevant today than it was when Mao first uttered it. Thus the best option for the United States is to help create incentives (and disincentives) that will encourage both Taipei and Beijing to maintain the undefined status quo—a middle ground between reunification and independence. Each side dislikes the current situation for its own reasons, but for both it is the best choice among unhappy alternatives.

The United States must use its diplomatic skill and military muscle to dissuade the PRC from continuing its coercive course toward Taiwan and persuade it to pursue a more constructive and conciliatory approach. Meanwhile, Washington should seek ways for Taiwan to participate in the international community while accepting the inevitable limitations of its indeterminate status.

The United States must also conduct more dialogue with key regional allies and friends, both to consider their views and to take the Taiwan situation out of its narrow bilateral context. Washington should focus on and publicize the hopeful signs of cultural interaction and commercial links between the two sides. At the same time, the United States must continue prudent contingency planning and maintain an active military presence in the region to sustain deterrence. It should also consider a more active diplomatic role to help facilitate future cross-strait discussions on political, military, and other issues.

For the past two decades, the essence of U.S. policy in the Taiwan Strait has been to preserve peace and stability in the region while indefinitely deferring the ultimate resolution of the problem. This approach has led to 20 years of prosperity and the proliferation of commercial contacts between Taiwan and the mainland. Yet today this stability shows unmistakable signs of strain. Unless both sides of the strait act creatively, Washington may find that the future it sought to postpone has already arrived. ☯

Painting China Green

The Next Sino-American Tussle

Elizabeth Economy

WHEN CHINESE PREMIER ZHU RONGJI meets President Bill Clinton and Vice President Al Gore in Washington in April, the political climate is unlikely to be auspicious. The United States and China have reached a virtual stalemate on each of their traditional agenda items. Negotiations over China's entry into the World Trade Organization have stalled; China's continued drive for reunification with Taiwan offers little potential for fruitful dialogue; and human rights remains an elusive area for compromise. Yet the Sino-American relationship may well define global prosperity and military security in the 21st century. Allowing it to deteriorate risks a future punctuated by frequent military and economic conflicts and global instability. Both sides are eager to sustain the illusion of progress produced by the recent presidential summits. Hence, a centerpiece of the talks will likely be a subject viewed by both as uncontroversial—environmental cooperation.

Chinese and American leaders believe that the environment is a low priority issue with plenty of common ground. This is a big mistake. The environment is as complex as other key diplomatic issues, featuring differing interests and priorities, weak Chinese institutions, Chinese defiance of international agreements, and conflict between Congress and the White House over how to achieve U.S. aims.

ELIZABETH ECONOMY is C.V. Starr Senior Fellow and Director of Asia Studies at the Council on Foreign Relations. She also served as Co-chair of the Woodrow Wilson Center's Working Group on Environment in U.S.-China Relations.

Moreover, environmental issues have direct and serious implications for other U.S. foreign policy objectives. A warmer Sino-American relationship is stymied by China's reluctance to seek any middle ground with the United States until it is in firm control domestically. But the environmental problems created by China's recent economic boom now threaten the country's fragile social, political, and economic infrastructure. This is a momentous issue, and the question is: Is China's economic growth sustainable? Progress in bilateral discussions rests on China's resolution of it. Fleeing to the environment as a short-term foreign policy sanctuary will be treacherous if these complications are ignored. If fully understood and thoughtfully addressed, however, China's environmental problems offer a unique opportunity for the United States to cooperate with China on a vital issue.

IT'S NOT EASY BEING GREEN

AT FIRST GLANCE, the connection between China's environment and U.S. interests may appear tenuous. China is halfway around the world and unlikely to affect American air and water quality. But China's impact on the global environment should not be underestimated. China is one of the world's largest contributors to both global climate change (albeit a distant second to the United States) and ozone depletion. Its environmental practices affect Americans, from the rate of skin cancer to agricultural productivity to the frequency and scale of natural disasters. Moreover, China's need for grain has a direct and growing impact on U.S. farmers' interests. Beyond these direct effects, however, China's environmental policy influences the full range of U.S. interests in China: stability and security, human rights, democracy, and trade.

The environment is beginning to shape China's economic and political choices in important ways. The government reports large internal migrations due to scarcities, particularly of water. These migrants will complicate Beijing's efforts to manage the overpopulated coastal cities, with their millions of unemployed workers. Moreover, political conflict over land and water resources has become endemic, occasionally erupting into wide-scale violence. Over the past few years, for example, farmers from the Ningxia Autonomous Region have raided the more fertile land in Inner Mongolia for a favored plant. Thousands of police and local officials have been injured by the incursions. China's environmental practices alone may not challenge economic growth, but when combined with other trends, their consequences for social stability are magnified. A China in political and economic disarray cannot be a stabilizing force in the region or the world.

Regarding human rights, China's environment causes both concern and hope. China's environmental problems encroach on the most basic necessities of life: clean air and safe drinking water. Every year, 300,000 Chinese citizens die prematurely from air pollution–related diseases. In 1996, 50,000 people were affected by water pollution–related diseases. Sixty million people cannot get enough clean water for their daily needs. But U.S. politicians should also recognize environmental action's potential to propel political change. In the environment, perhaps more than in any other area, the Chinese government has opened the political space for dissent. Rather than devote significant financial resources to environmental protection (it spends slightly under one percent of GDP), the government has permitted the emergence of genuine nongovernmental organizations (NGOs) devoted to the environment. Helped by the media and the general public, which also discuss environmental policy with unusual openness, these NGOs criticize and expose the weaknesses of local environmental protection efforts. Grassroots environmental organizations have blossomed, many of them dominated by politically reform-minded Chinese intellectuals.

Finally, as the United States attempts to reduce its growing trade imbalance with China, it should not overlook the sale of technologies and products protecting the environment. The World Bank estimates that between 1995 and 2004, China will require about $100 billion of infrastructural investment in water conservation, treatment, and sanitation. The market for environmental goods and services, already estimated at around $4 billion, is growing rapidly. American companies, however, still lag far behind their Japanese competitors in market share.

CHINA'S FAUSTIAN BARGAIN

CHINESE LEADERS KNOW they have a problem. They also realize that it is not just an environmental issue but an economic and political one. They have gambled that the rate of economic growth will outpace the rate of environmental degradation and resource scarcity. But their development practices have produced a costly environmental disaster; it is clear to anyone living in China that economic growth has come at the expense of the environment. The country's overwhelming reliance on coal has resulted in some of the world's worst air quality and acid rain that is damaging one-third of Chinese agricultural land. Eighty percent of wastewater and sewage is dumped untreated into rivers and lakes; in 1997, China's Environmental Protection Agency announced that water quality had deteriorated in every single major river system during the previous year. Fully 86 percent of the water in rivers flowing through China's cities is considered unsuitable for drinking or fishing.

This damage is haunting China's economic growth. Economists estimate the cost of environmental degradation and resource scarcity to be 8 to 12 percent of China's GDP. According to the World Bank, water scarcity and pollution alone annually cost China about $14 billion in lost industrial output and about $24 billion in crop loss. The health costs of air pollution will skyrocket—reaching $98 billion by 2020.

Perhaps the most dramatic example of the costs of China's decision to trade the environment for economic growth was 1998's flooding of the Yangtze River. Official indifference and decades of poor environmental choices—failing to protect wetlands and clear-cutting forests for timber, farmland, and industrial development—contributed to the unrelenting floods, which killed more than 3,000 people, destroyed 5 million homes, and inundated 52 million acres of land. The economic losses are estimated at more than $20 billion.

In the race between development and the environment, Chinese leaders have bet on development. Either because it had no choice—since the regime's legitimacy is predicated on continued rapid economic growth—or because it has decided to see who will blink first, China has placed the burden of global environmental problems on the rest of the world. Issues such as global climate change and ozone depletion are more diffuse and long-term than China's current woes. Chinese officials have resisted devoting financial resources to problems that they could blame on industrialized countries, a philosophy best summed up as "For China to play, the world must pay."

Elizabeth Economy

THE SILVER LINING

DESPITE THESE OBSTACLES, the silver lining of the April summit is that the environment may finally receive the attention it deserves. The danger lies in assuming that environmental discussions should provide no more than an easy photo opportunity for Gore and Zhu. The Clinton administration tends to settle for nonsubstantive policy "wins"—in the words of one official, "find[ing] the low hanging fruit"—rather than fighting for difficult new programs. Congress, in turn, blocks substantive initiatives by withholding funding without offering constructive alternatives. The United States cannot afford this repeat performance. China now stands on a precipice of change as steep as that in 1979, when the leadership launched its economic reform program. Since then, China has embarked on wholesale economic restructuring, including a national infrastructure program, that will not only determine its own economic and environmental future but will also affect the world's. Washington must acknowledge that changing Beijing's environmental performance will take several decades. As with other contentious issues in the Sino-American relationship, from intellectual property rights to control over weapons technology transfers, China's capacity to enforce its environmental agreements is constrained by bureaucratic and regional conflicts. The United States must act quickly if it is to influence China's choices.

First, Gore needs to incorporate businesses, foundations, and NGOs from both countries into the U.S.-China Forum on Environment and Development. The forum, which Gore inaugurated in April 1996, serves as the umbrella for cooperation between both countries' bureaucracies. The low level of funding to date—less than $10 million in 1997—has limited joint ventures to small-scale workshops on topics such as natural disaster relief, water usage, and energy efficiency. Introducing new actors into the forum will provide fresh sources of funding and expertise, organize the disparate efforts of environmental organizations in China, advance U.S. trade interests, and nonthreateningly support Chinese NGOs. Forum-sponsored projects should address both U.S. priorities like global climate change and Chinese domestic needs. Ventures could involve reforestation, energy efficiency, and renewable energy.

Painting China Green

Second, the United States urgently needs to soften China's recalcitrance on global climate change. Chinese leaders resist even minimal voluntary limits on greenhouse gas emissions for fear that more significant future commitments will slow China's economic development. Since Congress is withholding funding for domestic global warming initiatives until it sees China and other developing countries move on this issue, the White House is desperate for progress. Yet it should resist the temptation to oversell any summit agreement. China's compliance will be weak because it lacks the will and capacity to address climate change, and the United States is bound to be disappointed. Instead, Washington should proceed along the two tracks that offer the best hopes for improving Beijing's performance. The bill proposed by Senators John Chafee (R-R.I.), Joseph Lieberman (D-Conn.), and Connie Mack (R-Fla.), which grants early action credit to companies that reduce greenhouse gas emissions, should be expanded to include actions undertaken in other countries. The administration should also refrain from high-profile demonstration projects unless they are funded by those whose business interests will profit. U.S. efforts should focus on activities with a long-term payoff, such as training Chinese officials and researchers in environmental planning and enforcement, rather than on projects with limited application elsewhere in China.

Third, it is time for Congress to clear the way for lifting sanctions on U.S. assistance programs to China imposed after Tiananmen Square. The U.S.-Asia Environmental Partnership, the Trade and Development Agency, and the Overseas Private Investment Corporation could all facilitate exports of environmental goods and services to China. For U.S. firms to compete, they need financial and organizational assistance. There is no rationale for maintaining sanctions that hurt only U.S. companies and limit American advancement of its own environmental interests.

GETTING IT RIGHT

DISCORD AND DISTRUST are hallmarks of the Sino-American relationship. Despite recent efforts by both U.S. and Chinese leaders to move beyond the current stalemate, little has been achieved. Domestic politics on both sides and weak institutions in China confound efforts to achieve compromise. Although both sides want China's emergence as a global power to proceed smoothly, neither is willing to forgo short-term interests for long-term gain.

In this rather bleak political climate, the environment offers a fresh start. Gore and Zhu have the opportunity to accomplish something significant. By addressing environmental protection Gore will also serve broader U.S. interests of human rights and democracy, U.S. business development, and international security. By influencing China's economic and environmental choices, the United States will fundamentally shape the China that will emerge in the 21st century. Ensuring that China becomes a constructive participant in the international system will take time. Progress on the environment, as on other issues, requires both sides to commit themselves to a long-term strategy of institution-building to enable China to meet its domestic challenges as well as its international obligations. This does not mean that the United States should allow China to ignore its commitments in the interim. But the United States is best served by engaging China and helping it develop the capacity to be a respected and effective international actor. America's interests in China are significant and growing. We should take the time to get the relationship right.@

China: The Forgotten Nuclear Power

Brad Roberts, Robert A. Manning, and Ronald N. Montaperto

A DECADE after the end of the Cold War, the world faces the risk of new strategic instability. Policymakers in Washington, Beijing, and Moscow are moving toward decisions that may unintentionally increase nuclear dangers. The heart of the problem lies in insufficient attention to the intersection of three policy currents: American missile defenses, U.S.-Russian nuclear diplomacy, and Chinese nuclear modernization. Unless all three are given full consideration, American decisions in coming months could lead China to initiate a major buildup of its nuclear forces, increase Sino-Russian strategic cooperation, and jeopardize both efforts at arms reduction and the effectiveness of any American missile defenses that are eventually deployed.

A lingering bipolar mindset has left China the forgotten nuclear power. It is time that Washington turned its eyes to the East and came to grips with the fact that over the next decade it will likely be China, not Russia or any rogue, whose nuclear weapons policy will concern America most. The People's Republic has been modernizing its

BRAD ROBERTS is Fellow at the Institute for Defense Analyses. ROBERT A. MANNING is a former C.V. Starr Senior Fellow and Director of Asia Studies at the Council of Foreign Relations. He currently serves as Senior Counselor for Energy, Technology & Science Policy with the United States Department of State." RONALD N. MONTAPERTO is Senior Research Professor at the National Defense University. The opinions expressed herein are their personal views.

modest nuclear arsenal for 20 years and will continue to do so regardless of the actions of other nations. But external developments will influence the final contours of China's nuclear modernization program. In fact, Western actions have already had some effect, and not for the better. The Gulf War and the air war over Kosovo, for example, reinforced Chinese worries that precision-guided conventional weapons could destroy China's existing nuclear second-strike capability.

Such concerns about the erosion of China's nuclear deterrent have been largely dismissed by Americans, whose debates about national missile defense (NMD) have centered instead on the emerging dangers of small-scale missile launches from countries such as North Korea or Iran. Apart from questions of technological feasibility, the greatest obstacle to the deployment of such defenses has been thought to be the negative effects they might have on U.S.-Russian arms control agreements. Yet Washington seems determined to proceed with NMD whether or not it can find some way to overcome the current disagreement with Russia on modifying the Anti-Ballistic Missile (ABM) Treaty.

Less often discussed is the fact that whatever Moscow's reaction will be, Beijing will almost certainly regard the plans for the deployment of NMD as a challenge to its own nuclear deterrent. As a result, Chinese decision-makers may even now have begun worst-case planning to offset what they perceive to be an emerging threat. It is high time, therefore, to take a close look at China's current strategic posture, nuclear doctrine, and arms control strategy.

THROUGH A GLASS, DARKLY

EXAMINING CHINA'S strategic posture poses a major challenge, because China is quite deliberately the least transparent of the acknowledged nuclear powers. The American government keeps its own assessments of China's arsenal tightly classified, and so discussion must proceed on the basis of the limited data available.

China exploded its first nuclear device in October 1964, and its first hydrogen bomb shortly thereafter. All told, China has conducted 45 nuclear weapons tests in 33 years—a number identical to Britain's, but far less than the 1,030 conducted by the United

States. Until recently, Beijing invested only modestly in its nuclear forces, and as a 1996 signatory of the Comprehensive Test Ban Treaty (CTBT), it has accepted constraints on its modernization efforts.

China's nuclear force is designed for two types of missions: medium- and long-range strategic strikes (to which approximately two-thirds of its warheads are devoted), and tactical uses including low-yield bombs, artillery shells, atomic demolition mines, and possible short-range missiles (together accounting for the remaining one-third). The core of the strategic force is composed of ballistic missiles, most of which are tipped with conventional warheads and have ranges suitable for use within Eurasia. Reportedly, about 20 missiles—a small fraction of the long-range strike force—are capable of reaching targets in the continental United States. Because the bulk of China's aging missile force is liquid-fueled, the missiles are on a low state of alert, with fuel, warheads, and missiles all stored separately. At present Beijing has no ability to launch "on warning"— that is, at short notice or once an attack has already begun—but this will change once it deploys more advanced missiles in years to come.

China's emphasis on land-based missiles has stemmed in part from its apparent lack of success in developing other long-range delivery systems. Although Beijing has pursued the ability to launch missiles from the sea for decades, its current force reportedly consists of only one submarine, armed with 12 medium-range Julang 1 ballistic missiles. China has also devoted some effort to developing a nuclear bomber capability. But for the moment its few bombers remain old, highly vulnerable, and unable to reach the continental United States. China therefore lacks the full strategic "triad" (made up of land-, sea-, and air-based weapons) enjoyed by the United States and Russia.

Aware of these deficiencies, Beijing is intent on modernizing its missile force to improve its range, payload, accuracy, and survivability. It wants to be better able to penetrate enemy defenses, to have more advanced command, control, and communication systems, and to gain the ability to attack space-based assets. The availability of advanced Russian technologies has expanded China's wish list to include alternative delivery techniques such as cruise missiles and new submarines with ballistic missile launching capability.

Brad Roberts, Robert A. Manning, and Ronald N. Montaperto

One of the first tangible results of the Chinese modernization program will be the deployment in the near future of the new, long-range DF-31 missile, which was successfully tested in August 1999. The solid-fueled, road-mobile DF-31 has a range of about 8,000 km and will be targeted primarily against Russia and Asia—though it will also be capable of attacking sites in northwestern America. A naval variant of the DF-31 is also planned, and a still-longer-range system, the DF-41, is under development. American analysts agree that China has long had the ability to equip its ballistic missiles to deliver multiple warheads but has chosen not to do so. They disagree, however, about whether China can target those multiple warheads independently—that is, whether China has true MIRV capability.

China's deployment of short- and intermediate-range missiles, meanwhile, is increasing, particularly in Fujian province across the strait from Taiwan. The reported number of missiles deployed there grew from about 20 in the mid-1990s to between 160 and 200 in early 1999, and it is estimated that the number might rise to between 500 and 650 within five years. These missiles are generally thought to be tipped with conventional warheads, although some reports indicate they could be given nuclear payloads.

THE MAXIMUM FOR THE MINIMUM

FROM ITS START in the 1960s, China's nuclear posture has been one of "minimum deterrence": a small number of missiles are deployed in a pattern designed to ensure that if attacked first, the country would still be able to inflict unacceptable damage on its opponent. Minimum deterrence calls for potential retaliatory strikes against large "value" targets such as cities; it differs from "limited deterrence," which implies some nuclear war-fighting capabilities. Beijing's doctrine has been essentially a defensive one, designed to preempt nuclear blackmail and to guarantee China a place at the councils of the major powers.

Strong evidence suggests that the utility of this long-standing doctrine is currently being questioned. Some Western observers, for example, interpret the modernization program as representing a shift from minimum to limited deterrence. Others see a differentiation and diversification of Chinese doctrine taking place, which would ultimately yield a credible minimum deterrent against the United States and Russia, a more aggressive posture of limited deterrence for China's theater (i.e. shorter-range) nuclear forces, and an offensively configured, war-fighting posture for its conventional missile force. The possibility of a military confrontation with Washington over Taiwan dominates this debate. Chinese analysts seem to have concluded that more nuclear muscle is needed to avoid being coerced, and Beijing apparently believes that advanced missile capabilities offer the prospect of leverage it can use to secure the island's reunification with the mainland.

How big China's nuclear force becomes is largely a matter of will, not capability. Beijing certainly has more than enough fissile material for a substantial increase in its nuclear arsenal. It can also afford a major expansion of its missile force. It is generally accepted that China could produce as many as a thousand new missiles, mostly short-range, within the next decade, and some reports indicate a Chinese capability to produce 10–12 new long-range intercontinental ballistic missiles (ICBMs) per year.

An active Chinese MIRV program, of course, would dramatically increase the number of deliverable warheads. The U.S. House of Representatives Select Committee on U.S. National Security and Military/Commercial Concerns with the People's Republic of China—the Cox Committee—concluded that China is capable of an "aggressive deployment of upward of 1,000 thermonuclear warheads on ICBMs by 2015." A recent unclassified National Intelligence Estimate, however, predicts a much smaller deployment amounting to tens of ICBMs capable of targeting the United States, including a few tens of more survivable, land- and sea-based mobile missiles with smaller nuclear warheads.

A DANGEROUS NEIGHBORHOOD

DURING THE 1950s and 1960s, China's nuclear program was driven by challenges from the Soviet Union and the United States. Today both countries remain a profound concern for Beijing, but it has new worries as well, such as the emerging nuclear and missile capabilities in South Asia. (Here, of course, China's long-standing nuclear assistance to Pakistan is partly responsible for the problem.) Beijing's protestations that increased Indian nuclear capabilities will not produce a change in China's nuclear posture ring hollow. If India's Agni missile is deployed on mobile systems, as appears likely, this will further complicate Chinese nuclear planning. And if India moves to build a substantial number of warheads, Beijing will almost certainly resize and restructure its own nuclear arsenal.

Japan is another important factor in Beijing's nuclear calculus. Over the last decade, China has alternately feared that Japan would be drafted into a U.S.-led containment strategy or would be driven by a diminished American regional presence to confront China with its own nuclear force. Any deployment of theater missile defenses in Japan could provoke China to increase the number of weapons targeted there, including those with nuclear warheads.

As for Russia, Chinese thinking is conflicted. First and foremost, China appreciates Russia as a key source of advanced technology. At the same time the Chinese also seem concerned that despite having signed a no-first-use agreement with them, Russia has subsequently elaborated conditions under which it would indeed consider a first strike. If Russia were to deploy enhanced strategic defenses to protect its nuclear forces, China would be even more inclined to enlarge its own nuclear forces in order to retain a secure retaliatory capability.

The Chinese are skeptical, meanwhile, about Washington's professed commitment to de-emphasizing nuclear weapons in its current and future defense policy. Beijing thinks that the Pentagon remains committed to the centrality of such weapons in U.S. strategy, and it interprets U.S. reluctance to embrace a no-first-use doctrine as an indication of American planning for the use of nuclear weapons preemptively. China believes that the United States has a huge current quantitative advantage in destructive capability and will be able to increase its qualitative lead, as well, thanks to its greater technological sophistication. Furthermore, China believes that since U.S. counterforce capabilities can eliminate most of China's current second-strike capability, the addition of even a thin U.S. missile defense system would usher in a world in which the United States could dictate terms.

China: The Forgotten Nuclear Power

American officials and pundits have given considerable thought to the problem of constructing a missile defense system large enough to neutralize any threat from North Korea or the Persian Gulf but not so large as to render current Russian forces useless. The missing ingredient in these calculations has been China, which poses a particular problem because the size of its nuclear missile force is much closer to that of the so-called rogues than it is to Russia's. Even a thin U.S. NMD system could be viewed by Beijing as degrading China's nuclear deterrent. A move toward such a system could therefore motivate the Chinese to adjust their strategy and doctrine to compensate, by building larger forces and developing countermeasures to overwhelm U.S. defenses. This in turn would probably cause the United States to shift toward thicker defenses, creating a spiral that could become, if not a full arms race, then at least a jog. The initial American move would thus end up complicating the very problem that missile defenses were supposed to solve.

Beijing's initial response to U.S. NMD planning was signaled by its October 1999 announcement of a program earmarking an additional $9.7 billion to boost its second-strike capabilities. If the United States proceeds to deploy some 200 interceptors at two national sites (including one in Alaska) in the context of agreed minor amendments to the ABM treaty, China may well conclude that ensured penetration will require a buildup of its own long-range missile force and possibly also the introduction of some MIRVs, along with other countermeasures. If the United States goes further and pursues a broad range of sea-, air-, and space-based missile defense systems, China may seek a far more substantial capacity for itself, one that would enable it to overwhelm both national and theater defenses with both conventional and nuclear missiles. And if the United States goes so far as to withdraw from the ABM treaty entirely, China is likely to embark on a full-scale drive for a far more powerful nuclear force, concluding that Russian and other critics have been correct in arguing that the United States has no intention of stopping with a thin defense aimed at rogues but intends to erect a strong defense against all comers.

Chinese rhetoric conveys Beijing's increasing wariness of American power and intentions—a wariness that has already had an impact on Beijing's defense investment strategy and its willingness to support Washington's policy initiatives in other areas. The future of the Chinese nuclear program, nevertheless, is still up in the air, with three possibilities particularly likely. The first would involve China's trying to preserve or restore minimum deterrence with the United States by increasing the number of its ICBMS and enhancing their effectiveness in penetrating defenses. The second would involve China's concentrating more on India, remaining committed to minimum deterrence globally while moving toward more robust limited-deterrence strategies at the theater level. And the third would involve China's choosing to develop and deploy a force powerful enough to inflict significant pain on all adversaries in nearly all situations; here China would embrace limited deterrence across the board.

Elements of all three scenarios are visible in Beijing's present activities. For example, ongoing research and development of longer-range missiles and defensive countermeasures suggests movement in the direction of the first option. Large-scale deployment of missiles capable of targeting China's regional neighbors suggests the second option (albeit with a small nuclear component). And movement toward the third option can be inferred from ongoing investments and research, development, and deployment programs.

From Washington's perspective, the best outcome would be for China's nuclear forces to stay small and composed only of single-warhead missiles. The United States should seek to reduce the Chinese threat to American friends and allies in the region and try to ensure that China's strategic modernization does not block progress in reducing the Russian arsenal. The United States also has an interest in deploying viable theater missile defenses where they seem necessary, while taking care that Beijing does not see such deployments as gratuitously provocative. Securing these interests will require an understanding between Washington and Beijing on mutual intentions, capabilities, and future requirements.

SQUARING THE TRIANGLE

THE OLD bipolar strategic model simply does not fit post–Cold War realities. In addition to obscuring an important Sino-Russian nuclear dynamic, the bipolar focus fails to acknowledge that at some point Washington and Moscow's build-downs will intersect with Beijing's buildup. Establishing longer-term security and stability will require that the United States recognize the inevitable interaction between any nuclear "floor" that the United States and Russia might establish (either inside or outside the ABM treaty) and the "ceiling" that China chooses to erect.

Is minimum deterrence among the three major powers feasible, and would it be stable? What new forms of arms racing might occur, involving not merely offensive weapons but defensive weapons and countermeasures as well? Even if the three powers somehow arrive at a common notion of offensive or defensive stability among themselves, how will this be affected by Chinese concerns over Indian nuclear forces? And how might Russia have to account for possible future proliferation along its southern periphery? These are the kinds of questions that the emerging strategic multipolarity forces us to ask.

China was generally opposed to arms control during the Cold War, seeing it as an instrument for preserving the hegemony of stronger powers. But this mindset has evolved in recent years, as has China's understanding of arms control issues. During the last decade China has signed the nuclear Nonproliferation Treaty (NPT), the Chemical Weapons Convention, and the CTBT. China also supports the negotiation of a ban on the production of fissile materials and has agreed to bring its technology export practices more fully into compliance with international norms. In 1997 it joined the Zangger Committee, which, under the NPT, coordinates nuclear export policies. It has taken steps to address U.S. concerns about missile and chemical proliferation as well. There is no question that its current arms control and nonproliferation practices are significantly closer to U.S. preferences than they were a decade ago.

Nevertheless, Washington remains justifiably concerned about the depth of China's commitment to these undertakings. Reports continue to surface of disturbing Chinese transfers of weapons-related technologies and materials, and American officials believe China is not fully in compliance with its obligations under the Biological and Toxic Weapons Convention, to which it acceded in 1984.

The truth is that Beijing's arms control policies are ambiguous and in flux. Beijing may see arms control as part of an integrated set of policies aimed at enhancing national security and international stability. It may also view arms control negotiations as a way to increase leverage in bilateral ties with Washington, or as part of a larger effort to impose constraints on American freedom of action. And finally, it remains possible that Beijing pursues arms control at the rhetorical level but not in a way that has any actual impact on military decisions.

TO THE BARGAINING TABLE?

ONE CONSISTENT FEATURE of Beijing's nuclear arms control policies over the years has been an avoidance of negotiated constraints on its modest arsenal. In the 1980s Beijing argued that it need not address arms control issues until the superpowers reduced their nuclear arsenals by 50 percent. When the United States and Russia then cut back by 60 percent, the Chinese switched to arguing that the Americans and the Russians should come down to China's level—roughly 400 warheads—before talks could commence. Today, with the United States and Russia continuing to build down and China modernizing, the old Chinese logic no longer applies, and the time is fast approaching for the United States to put China's intentions to the test.

The current environment, it is true, does not appear favorable for the negotiation of sweeping new formal arms control accords. China sees the American drift toward missile defense as irreversible, and thus is unlikely to accept any restraint on its missile forces. The United States, meanwhile, is unlikely to accept restraints itself, not least because it has not yet decided what role it wants nuclear weapons to play in its own post–Cold War defense strategy. Yet the real possibility that uncoordinated decisions by Washington, Moscow, and Beijing could set off new, unintended, offensive versus defensive arms competition makes some kind of high-level discussions on the subject imperative.

At a minimum, Washington needs to rethink its nuclear and missile defense policies to take Chinese concerns and possible reactions into account. American policymakers, for example, have yet to analyze how effective their planned national missile defenses may be if China implements MIRVs, adds several hundred warheads, or obtains better penetration aids, countermeasures, and targeting assistance from Russia.

The United States should also go further and try to reach some understanding with China about what the conditions might be for strategic stability in the Sino-U.S. relationship and how to handle regional proliferation and arms control issues in areas such as the Korean Peninsula, South Asia, and the Middle East. China may just prefer an open-ended nuclear modernization program to any framework that the United States suggests. But by not putting Chinese intentions to the test, American policymakers risk ending up with the worst of both worlds: missile defenses that are less effective than they might have been, and Chinese and Russian strategic responses that leave the United States less secure than before.☯

China's HIV Crisis

Bates Gill, Jennifer Chang, and Sarah Palmer

THE PRICE OF PROSPERITY

"To get rich is glorious," the late Chinese leader Deng Xiaoping once exhorted his people. Defending this reformist vision, he added, "If you open the window for fresh air, you have to expect some flies to blow in." In the two decades of breakneck economic development since China's embrace of *gaige kaifang* (reform and opening), both the promise and the peril of Deng's two maxims have become abundantly clear. Although China enjoys growing wealth, increasing per capita incomes, and rising living standards, it also suffers from environmental degradation and a host of social ills including political unrest, increased crime, and a fraying social safety net. China, like other developing nations, faces tough choices between the benefits and the costs of modernity.

Unfortunately for China, however, the very nature of its particular political, social, and economic systems exacerbates the dangers of opening up. The growing problem of HIV/AIDS in China is a glaring example of this phenomenon, and one with enormous implications. Once dismissed by Chinese officialdom as a Western problem, the spread of HIV/AIDS has only recently gained serious attention from Beijing. But it may be too late: China now faces a major epidemic, one that the government will find extremely difficult to combat.

BATES GILL is Senior Fellow in Foreign Policy Studies at the Brookings Institution. JENNIFER CHANG is a Research Assistant in the Foreign Policy Studies Program at the Brookings Institution. SARAH PALMER is a virologist at the HIV Drug Resistance Program, National Cancer Institute, National Institutes of Health.

China's HIV Crisis

AFTER YEARS of neglect, the Chinese government has now begun to recognize the enormity of the country's HIV/AIDS problem. In June 2001, the Chinese health minister, Zhang Wenkang, made a stunning announcement while attending the United Nations General Assembly Special Session on HIV/AIDS: China could have as many as 600,000 cases of HIV. This admission stands in stark contrast to previous official statistics, which in 2000 counted only 22,517 registered cases. Even the higher numbers are suspect, for both practical and political reasons. The U.N. AIDS program (UNAIDS) estimates that there are more than one million people infected with HIV in China—and this figure might be even two or three times larger. Among mainland China's 22 provinces, serious HIV epidemics are already raging in 7, and threatening to break out in another 9. UNAIDS warns that the disease, if left unchecked, could afflict 20 million Chinese by 2010.

In certain parts of China the problem is already particularly acute. Along China's southern borders with the opium-growing regions of Burma, Thailand, and Laos, widespread intravenous (IV) drug use was an early source of HIV infection. Drug use—and with it the spread of HIV—has also extended along drug trafficking routes into China's northwestern province of Xinjiang. And it appears that the central province of Henan, China's second most populous, has been hit the hardest. According to some experts in international nongovernmental organizations (NGOS), as many as 1.2 million people in Henan are HIV-positive, largely owing to an unsafe blood collection system. Chinese and Western news media reports have focused in particular on "HIV/AIDS villages" in Henan where up to 80 percent of inhabitants have contracted the virus, and more than 60 percent already suffer from AIDS.

According to the health minister's speech at the United Nations, China's HIV caseload is increasing at 30 percent a year, although a later report by Deputy Health Minister Yin Dakui said that new cases actually increased by 67 percent in the first six months of 2001. Even accepting lower government estimates for infections and their annual growth, China will harbor some 6.4 million cases of HIV/AIDS in 2010, and even Health Minister Zhang has acknowledged that the number could rise to 10 million if the infection rate increases significantly. By comparison, in the United States, where the disease was detected nearly 20 years ago, there are today an estimated 900,000 people living with HIV/AIDS, and an additional 40,000 new cases are reported each year. Even the most conservative projections for China will easily place it among the world's most heavily HIV-infected nations within the next five to ten years.

How did this crisis emerge, and what can be done about it? What may have begun as a "foreign" disease has now swept through China. This is largely due to recent, dramatic changes in demography and social mores in the country, as well as deteriorating health care practices. Seen in this light, China's spreading HIV/AIDS problem is becoming both a cause and a consequence of the country's socioeconomic transformation. Given that the government is both unaccustomed and increasingly unable to respond to a health care crisis of this magnitude, the problem will certainly get much worse before its gets any better.

LOST BOYS (AND GIRLS)

DURING the Maoist era, the *hukou* system of household registration bound people to either the rural village or the urban area where they lived. Few could successfully evade the *hukou* system, because of a strict rationing and coupon system for food and other basic items. But in today's China, freedom of movement has increased enormously. The most dramatic expression of this mobility is the "floating population" (*liudong renkou*): an estimated 100 million itinerants who have left their official residence—typically in the poorer countryside—to seek a better living in urban areas, but without the benefit of official assistance in housing subsidies, health care, or education. Adding to this group, many of the 40 million, mostly urban workers laid off in recent years from failing state-owned enterprises are also now on the move, in search of a decent living.

These large numbers of roaming workers will become one of the most significant sources of new HIV infections in China over the coming years. The floating population is largely composed of young to middle-aged men and women, persons in their most sexually active stages of life. According to a survey in the mid-1990s, 81 percent of floating workers are between 15 and 45 years old, with over half of them between 20 and 30 years old. The very nature of the floating population renders it difficult to monitor, educate, and treat. Many of its members are poorly educated, illiterate, or speak only non-Mandarin dialects, making it all the more difficult for health care workers to target them effectively. As undocumented and unregistered citizens, they must live a semi-clandestine existence beyond the reach of officialdom; because of their willingness to take on low-paying or illicit employment disdained by city-dwellers, they are often alienated from society. If these workers run into legal or financial trouble and are forced to return home or move elsewhere, the HIV carriers among them can spread the infection wherever they go.

To make matters worse, IV drug abuse among this group is on the rise—as it is throughout much of China. The despair and dislocation brought on by economic hardship helps explain why many Chinese have turned to drugs. But drug use is not restricted to marginalized or socially disaffected groups. More and more urban youths also now have access to illegal drugs. As a consequence of the one-child policy, many children are indulged by their parents and by two sets of grandparents with money and freedom, both of which can be used to experiment with drugs. This augurs ill for China's HIV epidemic. In the recent past, IV drug use was seen as the principal source of HIV infection in China, with the government estimating that some 70 percent of HIV-positive individuals are IV drug users. Although drug use may not have been the initial cause of infection in all these cases, the sharing of needles is a highly efficient mode of transmission. With the Chinese government claiming there are some 860,000 drug addicts in China—probably an underestimate—this group will continue to be a significant contributor to the country's HIV/AIDS problem.

COURTING RISK

THE FOCUS on drug users, however, distorts public perceptions as to who faces a high risk of contracting HIV. Although IV users constitute the largest proportion of HIV cases in China today, the fastest growing cause of the disease's spread in the country is unprotected sex within the heterosexual population. Beijing's statistics claim that less than 10 percent of HIV infections are attributable to heterosexual intercourse (and an even smaller percentage is linked to homosexual sex). But with more than 700 million Chinese aged between 15 and 49, public health specialists can readily envision a major epidemic spreading among the heterosexual population alone. Casual and premarital sex has increased markedly in China. A 2001 survey on attitudes toward sex and marriage showed that only 27 percent of young respondents, as opposed to 84 percent of people in their parents' generation, believe that an individual's first sexual experience should occur after marriage.

This boom in promiscuity has been further fueled by China's resurgent commercial sex industry. Like widespread drug use, prostitution was thought to have been all but eradicated under the stringent societal norms of Maoist China. However, the opening of Chinese society in the 1980s demonstrated that the sex trade, as old as Chinese civilization itself, had never fully disappeared and was reemerging in full force. Today, Chinese police estimate that there are around four million prostitutes in the country.

This expansion in commercial sex work owes to forces both old and new. Growing income disparities, poverty among women, labor mobility, and consumerism all contribute. So does the increasing consumerism and commodification of modern life in China, which produces a parallel commodification of women. For many Chinese men, having a second wife or mistress has become a status symbol, much like owning a car or a cellular phone. It also comports with practices of the not-so-distant past, when it was common for monied Chinese men to marry more than one wife. Furthermore, business-related entertaining involving prostitutes has become standard practice in some quarters. A recent report on self-employed entrepreneurs (*getihu*), a growing social class in China, found that "*getihu* young men are frequently identified as spreading [sexually transmitted infections] and engaging in HIV-related risk-taking sexual practices." Meanwhile, the spread of new technologies, such as pagers and cell phones, is allowing commercial sex workers to move out of traditional red-light districts, promoting a further spread of sexually transmitted diseases while also complicating regulation and preventive education. Numerous epidemiological studies have demonstrated the steady spread of HIV through China's population of prostitutes. From there, HIV goes into the general population (or is circulated back to previously uninfected sex workers) via clients who pass the virus to their spouse or other sex partners in mainland China and beyond.

Take, for example, the town of Dongguan. Located in Guangdong province and near the border with Hong Kong, Dongguan is home to an estimated 300,000 women sex workers. These women—mostly from poor inland or northeastern provinces—mainly serve Hong Kong businessmen who regularly shuttle to the mainland. Similar enclaves on the coast of Fujian province cater to Taiwanese businessmen who frequent nightclubs, beauty parlors, massage parlors, and karaoke bars that also provide sexual services.

Another source of the spread of HIV in China is homosexual intercourse, especially among men. Some estimates place the number of gay men in China at between five and seven percent of the male population. As China grows more liberal, homosexuality is more openly expressed and tolerated. It was only recently removed from China's official list of psychiatric disorders, and reports suggest that local law enforcement has reduced crackdowns on gay bars and clubs in larger Chinese cities. Fortunately, such tolerance may have beneficial effects on the spread of HIV. If it means that China's gay community is no longer driven underground, anti-HIV awareness, prevention, and treatment programs might more readily reach this vulnerable population.

TRADITIONS AND TABOOS

ALTHOUGH dramatic socioeconomic transformation has exacerbated the spread of HIV/AIDS in China, the persistence of long-standing traditions and taboos is another contributing factor. Take, for instance, the deeply ingrained cultural preference for male children. One of the most startling demographic trends in China is the growing divide between the number of males and females born each year. The natural ratio of males to females born each year is about 105 to 100. However, according to Tyrene White, a scholar at Swarthmore

College, China's ratio in 1995 was 117.4 boys for every 100 girls, and in 1997 it was skewed even further to 120 males for every 100 females. Figures compiled by the CIA show an imbalance that is not as great, but still dramatic: in the Chinese population aged under 15, the ratio is about 110 to 100. Even this disparity means that over the next decade some 15 million Chinese men will come of age with bleak prospects for finding female partners, let alone wives.

The rapid socioeconomic changes of the 1980s and 1990s, combined with the one-child policy, have tended to reinforce this traditional preference for male heirs who carry on the family name, are expected to take care of aging parents, and tend to bring in more income. Now that ultrasound technology allows parents to identify the gender of their child before birth, sex-selective abortions, although illegal, are further altering the makeup of Chinese society. The consequent dearth of available brides fuels demand for commercial sex workers, helps accelerate male migration into cities, and increases the numbers of women who are kidnapped and sold into prostitution or as "unwilling brides."

A traditional conservatism in China also makes it difficult to have frank and open discussions on sex-related topics, which in turn stymies anti-HIV education and other preventive measures. Schools do not have formalized sex education, which explains why so many Chinese youth know very little about sexually transmitted diseases. A recent survey of 4,000 Chinese showed that fewer than four percent of them understood what HIV and AIDS are and how HIV is transmitted; more than half believe that sharing utensils with HIV carriers can transmit the disease. Such ignorance about HIV transmission also results in the stigmatization of people with the disease, which forces the problem deeper into the shadows. Not only do infected individuals feel alienated in their hometowns, but they may even be rejected by their own families. Making matters worse, there is even a great deal of ignorance in China's public health sector, as illustrated by the many cases of hospitals and clinics refusing to treat afflicted patients.

Public education could make a big difference. Thailand, which has a well-developed sex industry, has been able to use education, government regulation, and preventive programs to help stem the spread of HIV. In contrast, although sexual mores in China are changing rapidly, attempts to increase HIV/AIDS awareness have met with strong conservative opposition. Moves to put condom machines on university campuses, for example, or to erect billboards promoting condom use have been harshly criticized.

BLOOD MONEY

A CULTURAL TABOO against blood donation also means that the country suffers from chronically low blood supplies. China has only about 0.8 milliliters of blood per capita available for transfusions, far below the World Health Organization recommendation of 7.0 milliliters. Unfortunately, the predisposition against donation also means that much of China's blood supply comes from blood sellers—typically a less safe source than voluntary donors. China has learned too late how easily HIV can be introduced into the general population through tainted blood transfusions.

The buying and selling of blood in China is a lucrative and poorly regulated enterprise. Although the nation's 1998 Blood Donation Law made blood selling illegal, the law of supply and demand guarantees continued collection schemes, now moved underground where regulation is virtually impossible. Reports in *Beijing Wanbao*, for example, tell of state-run factory workers who, when given mandatory blood donation quotas to meet, paid dealers known as *xuetou*, or "bloodheads," to find migrant workers who "donated" blood in their stead. Until the supply of voluntarily donated blood more closely meets domestic demand, such schemes will be difficult to wipe out.

The transmission of HIV from illegal blood sales has received considerable coverage in the Chinese and Western news media. In circumstances now routinely repeating themselves in parts of rural China, poor farmers in the late 1980s and early 1990s were lured by cash to sell their blood to bloodheads. In some cases, bloodheads enticed entire villages of hundreds of adults to sell their blood or plasma for between 40 and 100 yuan (about $5 to $12) each. Poor peasants, otherwise making the equivalent of two or three hundred dollars per year, eagerly sold their blood, in some cases over the course of months and years, to supplement their meager incomes. Few of them had ever heard of HIV or AIDS. Those who did know about it considered it a "Western disease" or a "rich people's disease" and probably asked few questions before selling their blood.

Selling blood plasma is particularly appealing. By selling plasma—instead of whole blood—sellers do not lose red blood cells, and thus believe they can sell more often without fear of anemia. After extraction, an individual's blood is often mixed with other sellers' blood of the same type and placed in a centrifuge. Plasma is then removed from the whole blood, and the remaining mixture of blood cells and platelets is reinjected into the donors. The entire process takes only about 30 minutes, and there are reports of people selling blood plasma as many as three times a day for five days or longer. But this method of pooling, reinjection, and multiple plasma sales means that blood-borne disease in one seller can easily infect dozens of others. Moreover—again as a cost-saving measure—syringes are commonly reused during the collection process. Blood collectors rarely screen sellers for HIV, hepatitis, or other blood-borne diseases, nor do they test the blood before selling it to hospitals or individuals in need of transfusions. Indeed, because of increasing health care costs in China, many people needing blood transfusions are advised to go directly to collection stations to purchase inexpensive blood, bypassing hospital screening altogether.

Tenacious health care workers, increasingly vocal HIV/AIDS sufferers, and Chinese and Western news media are beginning to unearth the disastrous effects of nearly a decade of illicit blood sales in the Chinese countryside. In response, many local officials have sought to conceal their involvement in these practices and to prevent reporters and government health care professionals from visiting villages and towns with HIV-infected residents. Central government health officials are unable to gauge the full extent of the HIV/AIDS situation in the countryside and rely almost entirely on village officers and their own informal networks for information about the prevalence of HIV and AIDS. Efforts by local officials to conceal incidents of HIV in the countryside not only deprive afflicted citizens of medical attention, but also foster the continued spread of the disease.

China's HIV Crisis

AILING HEALTH CARE

THE TRAGEDY of blood-selling schemes are part of a larger problem: China's failing health care system. Economic pressures have forced the state to cut back on its traditional role as the country's sole health care provider, leaving a largely unregulated vacuum in its place. Although wealthy Chinese can access state-of-the art medical technologies, hundreds of millions no longer have even basic medical care, especially in the countryside. In 1978, some 20 percent of the national health budget was spent on rural areas, but this figure had been slashed to 4 percent by the mid-1990s. Less than one-tenth of China's 900 million peasants have any form of health insurance, yet health care costs have increased enormously, and local clinics have closed their doors because they cannot compete in the market economy. Hardest hit by these changes is the urban floating population. Not only do they risk contracting HIV and other diseases, but, living in shanties on construction sites or on the edges of cities, they lack even basic health services and are highly unlikely to receive any form of preventive education or treatment.

Chinese health care professionals emphasize that although HIV testing is now widely available, albeit sometimes for a hefty fee, few HIV-positive patients can afford the cost of anti-HIV drugs produced by Western pharmaceutical companies. (In North America, a carefully prescribed and monitored "drug cocktail" regimen costs between $15,000 and $30,000 a year.) Some major drug companies have announced that they will cut prices of anti-HIV drugs sold in China, and the Chinese government is launching an effort to negotiate even lower prices. But although such measures will help, the vast majority of anti-HIV therapies available today were designed to combat strains of HIV found predominantly in Western Europe and North America, and may not be as effective against HIV strains prevalent in China. For both these reasons, doctors are forced to focus on the symptoms of HIV/AIDS— such as coughs, fever, skin lesions, stomach ailments, and pneumonia— but are unable to slow the infection's fatal course. In remote rural areas, afflicted individuals might go without even this most basic care.

As with blood collection, another problem is the reuse of needles and syringes, particularly since many medications in China are administered by injection. A large underground market exists for used needles, which are cleaned, repackaged, and resold to hospitals and clinics in other provinces. To save money, some clinics also reuse needles and syringes themselves. Such unsanitary injections are rapidly spreading blood-borne diseases such as hepatitis B and C, and some experts believe that they will become one of the main modes of HIV transmission in the future.

TOO LITTLE, TOO LATE?

FOREIGN PUBLIC HEALTH OFFICIALS see the potential for a disastrous convergence of the three main paths of HIV transmission in China: from the southern border regions, the spread of HIV largely through intravenous drug use; from the eastern seaboard, the spread of HIV through sexual contact; and from the central inland provinces, the spread of HIV through illicit and unsafe blood collection. Beijing has also taken note and began to take some action in the late 1990s. As early as 1996, the central government established a commission to coordinate the national response to HIV/AIDS in China, and in 1998 and again in 2001 issued formal action plans. But it was not until late 2001 that the government began to make a serious and public effort to combat the disease. According to the health minister, funding to combat HIV/AIDS increased to about 100 million yuan (around $12 million) annually in 2001 and national bonds amounting to 950 million yuan have been issued for the improvement of blood bank services. China has also established a national-level Center for AIDS Prevention and Control within the Chinese Academy of Preventative Medicine, under the Ministry of Health.

Following the dramatic revelation of China's HIV/AIDS crisis in mid-2001, a number of other high-profile steps were taken. China held its first international AIDS conference in November 2001, with some 2,000 participants from 20 countries. Generally speaking, the official media in China has been increasingly free to write and broadcast about HIV/AIDS. On World AIDS Day, December 1, in addition to large government-sponsored education events in China's major cities, China Central Television broadcast a cautionary play in prime time about a businessman who contracts HIV through casual, heterosexual sex. Emulating other Asian countries such as Thailand, China has apparently begun to test its new military recruits, typically teenage males from poorer rural areas, for HIV infection. The government has also taken steps to provide special care to victims of HIV in the country's most notorious "AIDS village," Henan's Wenlou. There are even a number of reports of courts granting compensation to HIV victims infected through faulty blood transfusions.

Looking ahead, Chinese authorities have issued some ambitious goals. Officials who organized last year's national AIDS conference have stated their aim of reducing the growth rate of HIV infection to 10 percent annually by 2005. In a recently released action plan, the Chinese health ministry forecast new and augmented funding through budget increases and the issuance of government bonds. But because such funds are still limited, they will go primarily to education, counseling, and cleaning up the country's blood-donation system. Beijing hopes that at least 75 percent of the urban and 45 percent of the rural populations will have a basic preventive understanding of HIV and its transmission by 2005, and that all health care providers will have on-the-job training concerning HIV/AIDS. The document also includes a call for raising condom usage to at least half the people in high-risk populations. Another goal is that at least 50 percent China's HIV victims should receive local treatment and care. But given the already advanced stage of the HIV epidemic in China, these targets seem extremely optimistic.

Many problems remain before China gets a handle on its HIV/AIDS crisis. Although there has been more official media coverage, the scandals of rural blood collection or the more general breakdown of China's health care system are rarely mentioned. Some investigative reporting by the quasi-independent *Nanfang Zhoumou* has revealed the abuses of blood collection schemes in Henan, but the newspaper's publishers have been pressured by provincial authorities to cut back on their coverage. HIV sufferers who do appear at conference venues or on television are typically not identified or are disguised, further contributing to the stigmatization of the disease. To fulfill its mission in educating the public and caring for victims, the Chinese Ministry of Health will require far greater governmental support and political clout. But even that is not enough. Since the spread of HIV/AIDS occurs at the grassroots, it needs to be addressed at that level. China, however, lacks the expertise and capital to focus on the grass-roots, and the authorities are wary of semi- or wholly autonomous organizations that might try to do so. The preference for Leninist "democratic centralism"—that is, a top-down, Communist Party–led approach—still prevails in China and complicates Beijing's ability to deal fully with its HIV/AIDS problem.

A TORTUOUS ROAD

To AVOID a looming health disaster, China's government and the international community must take more aggressive action. Aside from the potentially monumental human cost, experience across the globe has also demonstrated the destabilizing social consequences of widespread HIV infection.

Given the scarcity of resources, anti-HIV efforts in China should focus on three major areas: education and awareness, improved health care, and intensified government oversight. Chinese public health professionals recognize that education and prevention are the most important near-term tactics. This approach should include a stronger focus on HIV/AIDS education and awareness, including the promotion of condom use and the introduction of sex education in schools. Providing better information will require improved epidemiological studies and enhanced monitoring of the disease's progression. HIV/AIDS awareness campaigns need to be targeted at the very venues where high-risk behavior occurs, such as teahouses, public bathhouses, barber shops, massage parlors, and nightclubs.

China's health care system also needs top-to-bottom improvements if the fight against HIV/AIDS is to succeed. Local public health officials should be given greater latitude to identify vulnerable populations and to establish appropriate clinics, prevention programs, and counseling centers. Health care providers also need to recognize and treat other sexually transmitted diseases, such as herpes and gonorrhea, which facilitate HIV infection, especially among high-risk groups such as commercial sex workers. And aggressive measures are needed to develop and implement high national standards for blood collection, organ donation, and the sanitary use of needles and other medical equipment.

The political context in which these steps unfold is equally important. Local and national laws and policies are needed to prevent discrimination against HIV victims, ensure the confidentiality of HIV testing and counseling, promote HIV awareness, encourage voluntary blood donation, and impose heavy, enforceable penalties on illicit blood-collection rackets. Government leaders need to devote more resources to this problem, not only through budget increases, but also by untangling bureaucratic obstacles so that health officials and practitioners, family planning agencies, the Education Ministry, the State Drug Administration, official media outlets, and public security bureaus will work more effectively together to combat HIV/AIDS. Overall, the Chinese leadership will need to place a far higher priority on HIV/AIDS prevention and treatment. Unfortunately, past experience suggests that China's political machine will not mobilize against a pervasive social problem (as with corruption), until one of its own high-level officials is openly affected.

The international community can do more as well. Many intergovernmental bodies, national governments, and NGOs from around the world have begun to provide expertise and financial resources to help China deal with its HIV/AIDS epidemic. For example, the World Bank recently loaned $250 million to support HIV prevention programs in four Chinese provinces, augmenting millions of dollars in anti-HIV assistance provided by Western governments. U.S. government cooperation has included two visits by delegations from the Centers for Disease Control and Prevention (CDC), and plans for exchanges between Chinese and U.S. specialists. According to CDC officials, potential collaborative programs in the future could focus on surveillance, epidemiological studies, education, blood safety, and community health care. The National Institute of Allergies and Infectious Diseases has also established collaborative programs with its Chinese counterparts. This list should be expanded to include other U.S. agencies such as the Food and Drug Administration and the National Cancer Institute. U.S.-China cooperation in combating HIV/AIDS stands out as a potentially positive area for bilateral relations.

Until very recently, denial and institutional inertia characterized the Chinese government's response to HIV/AIDS. When the first cases were reported in the mid-1980s, the government immediately treated the problem as a public security issue, blaming foreigners, prostitutes, drug users, and minorities for introducing the disease into China. Only recently has the government realized that attempts to isolate and purge infected individuals simply drives the problem further underground. For the Chinese government and those foreign agencies wishing to help, the first matter of business will be an accurate assessment of the actual magnitude of the crisis. But accepting that there is a problem is only the first step on a tortuous road to containing the epidemic. China must also learn to balance the perils and the promise of increased modernization and openness.

Ties That Bind

Joseph P. Quinlan

RETHINKING U.S.-CHINA TRADE

U.S.-CHINA trade relations have been on a fast track since the two countries signed a historic trade agreement in November 1999. That accord culminated nearly 15 years of difficult negotiations and helped pave the way for U.S. congressional approval of permanent normal trade relations with Beijing in 2000. Last year, further agreements in such sensitive sectors as agriculture, retail, and insurance were hammered out, facilitating the deal of all deals: China's entry into the World Trade Organization (WTO).

Notwithstanding this success at the bargaining table, the heavy lifting of U.S. trade negotiations will not do much to dent the outsized U.S. trade deficit with China, which topped $80 billion in 2001. While the negotiators were talking, the ground beneath U.S.-China commercial relations was shifting. Over the past decade, shallow links based on trade have been transformed into a more complex relationship shaped by rising U.S. foreign direct investment (FDI) and sales by U.S. foreign affiliates in China. Mirroring the global norm, sales by these affiliates, rather than U.S. exports, have become the preferred way to deliver American products to the Chinese market. As a result, U.S. export figures—which do not count these affiliate sales—understate the true level of commercial engagement between the two countries.

Meanwhile, more U.S. multinational corporations are using China as an export platform in the face of unrelenting global competition. An increasing percentage of the products these affiliates export from China is destined for the U.S. market. These goods count as Chinese exports to the United States—even though they

---

JOSEPH P. QUINLAN is Senior Global Economist at Morgan Stanley.

are shipped by U.S.-owned entities—and they contribute to the ever-widening American trade deficit. European and Japanese multinationals are following a similar strategy of manufacturing in China for export, further adding to America's import bill from that country. Together, the delivery of U.S. goods through affiliates and the increasing use of the mainland as an export base by the world's leading multinational corporations could inhibit any significant improvement in the American trade deficit with China.

Despite this stubbornly large trade deficit, U.S. policymakers must recognize just how much successful trade negotiations have enhanced market access to China. Many U.S. firms, in both manufacturing and services, are poised to reap the windfall of a more open Chinese market. But increased market penetration does not necessarily imply a corresponding reduction in the U.S. trade deficit with China. American firms prefer to leverage their global core competencies through FDI rather than through trade, particularly in such a strategic and competitive market as China. Failing to understand this dynamic will only fuel resentment in Washington and heighten the risks of errors when crafting policy toward Beijing, possibly even provoking a protectionist backlash. If the relationship between the United States and China is destined to be among the most important in the world, then American policymakers must rethink how the two countries do business with each other.

GREAT LEAP OUTWARD

ALTHOUGH open to the West for the past quarter-century, China really emerged on corporate America's radar screen only in the past decade. Through the early 1990s, U.S.-China commercial ties were relatively underdeveloped and based almost exclusively on trade. Despite a fourfold increase in trade between the two economies in the 1980s, more than three-quarters of it in 1990 consisted of U.S. imports from China. Meanwhile, U.S. exports to the mainland remained modest, at around one percent of the U.S. total.

Even more indicative of underdeveloped links with China, U.S. investment roots there were virtually nonexistent ten years ago. American FDI in China was less than $400 million in 1990, among the smallest of all U.S. investment positions in Asia. Fewer than 50 majority-owned U.S. foreign affiliates were operating there, and they employed a mere 13,600 workers out of a global U.S. affiliate work force of nearly 7 million. With such a minuscule investment base, U.S. foreign affiliate sales in China tallied just $775 million in 1990, compared to a global total of $1.2 trillion. Affiliate sales within China accounted for less than 15 percent of total American exports to the mainland—at a time when global affiliate sales of U.S. firms were more than double total U.S. exports. In sum, U.S.-China commercial relations were "shallow," or trade-based, as opposed to "deep," or based on both trade and investment.

But commercial relations entered a new phase in 1993. Inland cities were opened up to foreign firms, and certain restrictions in such sectors as power generation and telecommunications services were lifted. Beijing began to reform its tax system and overhaul the exchange-rate regime. Encouraged by a more liberal investment environment, foreign firms gained greater access to the local market and tighter control over how to structure their mainland operations. American firms responded by sinking more capital into China in 1993–94 ($1.8 billion) than during the preceding 12 years combined. Amid the quickening pace of reform and China's robust growth, the number of U.S. foreign affiliates on the mainland nearly tripled between 1993 and 1995—as did the number of Chinese workers on U.S. affiliate payrolls.

Thanks to this new opening, the pace of U.S. FDI in China accelerated over the second half of the 1990s. American investment flows to China rose by an annual average of $1.3 billion in 1996–2000, up from an average annual increase of $365 million in 1990–95. Of the $8.7 billion that U.S. firms invested in China between 1990 and 2000, roughly 75 percent occurred from 1996 on. Including Hong Kong, the strategic gateway that many U.S. firms use to access the mainland, China became a preferred location for American business not only in Asia but among developing nations in general. Among the latter, only Mexico (a partner in the North American Free Trade Agreement) and Brazil (which undertook large-scale privatization sales) attracted more U.S. investment than China and Hong Kong did in the second half of the 1990s.

The rapid American investment buildup in China after 1996 stands in stark contrast to the halting pace of trade talks over the same

U.S. Sales in China, 1990–99

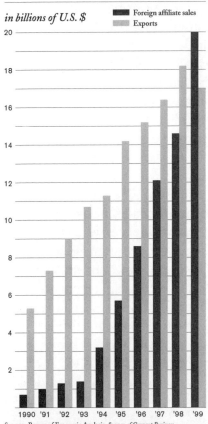

in billions of U.S. $

■ Foreign affiliate sales
▨ Exports

20 ─────
18 ─────
16 ─────
14 ─────
12 ─────
10 ─────
8 ─────
6 ─────
4 ─────
2 ─────

1990 '91 '92 '93 '94 '95 '96 '97 '98 '99

SOURCE: Bureau of Economic Analysis, *Survey of Current Business*, "Operations of U.S. Multinational Companies: Preliminary Results from the 1999 Benchmark Survey" (March 2002) and "U.S. International Services: Cross-Border Trade in 2000 and Sales Through Affiliates in 1999" (November 2001).

period. The U.S. trade deficit with China rose from $10.4 billion in 1990 to nearly $70 billion in 1999, heightening the impression that China was playing by its own rules at the expense of U.S. jobs and income. As the trade deficit rose, so did the animosity in Washington.

But while negotiators were talking, U.S. firms were investing in China. Total assets of U.S. multinationals there ballooned from $2.1 billion in 1990 to nearly $33 billion by 1999. By the end of the decade, the number of U.S. majority-owned foreign affiliates in China topped 450, up from just 45 in 1990. American firms employed some 262,000 workers, one of the largest affiliate work forces in developing Asia. More assets, more operations, and more workers meant more U.S. foreign affiliate sales. In fact, total sales by U.S. majority–owned affiliates exploded in the 1990s, rising from $775 million in 1990 to $20 billion in 1999. (U.S. exports of goods and services also rose sharply over the same period—by roughly 220 percent—but not nearly at the same pace as affiliate sales.) Once U.S. minority–owned affiliates are factored in, affiliate sales totaled $23 billion in 1999. That year marked a new zenith in U.S.-China relations and capped a remarkable decade of bilateral integration, as U.S. affiliate sales exceeded exports for the first time.

Thanks to the growing American presence in China, the greater Chinese market (comprising Hong Kong and the mainland) is now the largest source of U.S. foreign-affiliate income among developing nations. Affiliate income from greater China rose more than sixfold during the 1990s, topping $7 billion in 2000; in 2001, the figure dipped but was still 18 percent higher than earnings from second-place Mexico. What that means is that, contrary to popular perception, China is now a source of considerable earnings for many U.S. firms. American lawmakers should not forget this as they debate and craft policies toward China. Nor should Washington lose sight of the fact that U.S.-China commercial relations are poised to enter a new phase following China's WTO accession.

MORE THAN A MARKET

U.S. MULTINATIONALS initially entered China to gain access to the mainland's large but untapped consumer market. In the early 1990s, reaching the Chinese consumer required "barrier-jumping" investment to overcome tariffs and other measures that discriminated against trade. Once inside China, U.S. foreign affiliates were largely independent (or stand-alone), with minimal links to the parent company. High transportation costs and trade restrictions hindered integration between parent firms and affiliates. Hence the bulk of what affiliates produced in China was not for export but for the local market. Accordingly, local sales by U.S. affiliates accounted for more than 90 percent of their total sales in 1990. That share then declined slightly but still hovered around 84 percent in 1995, well above the global average of 67 percent.

Today, access to the Chinese consumer remains a key motivation of U.S. multinationals. Customer proximity is critical in a country as fragmented as China. The mainland is not a unified market but a collection of markets with different dialects and varying levels of development, infrastructure, and per capita income. These variables, along with high levels of brand sensitivity, interprovincial barriers, and cost- and quality-control issues, dictate that U.S. firms adapt to local tastes and market conditions. Coca-Cola's mantra to "think local, act local" helps explain that company's long track record of success in China.

But China has become more than just a market to U.S. firms. As the country's investment policies and economic conditions changed over the past decade, so did the strategies of U.S. multinationals. By the mid-1990s, American firms had moved beyond the stand-alone affiliate strategies. Market-seeking investment was increasingly complemented by efficiency-seeking investment as more U.S. firms turned to the mainland as a low-cost manufacturing base in the face of mounting global competition. Cheap labor, falling transportation costs, and more liberal economic policies allowed firms to outsource more functions and transfer more activities to their affiliates. Meanwhile, U.S. parent-affiliate linkages became tighter and more intricate. This increased integration was centered largely on labor-intensive production and the manufacturing of goods for both the local market and for export.

Taken together, these developments altered the direction of affiliate sales. Whereas affiliate sales to the local Chinese market rose more than fivefold between 1994 and 1999, affiliate exports to the United States rose more than twelvefold, soaring to $2.7 billion in 1999, according to the U.S. Bureau of Economic Analysis (BEA). Exports to third markets rocketed up as well—likely reflecting rising shipments through Hong Kong—and hit $3.5 billion in 1999, up from $500 million in 1994. Figures from the U.S. Census Bureau show a large increase in affiliate trade over the past half-decade as well: related-party imports from China to the United States, or affiliate shipments to their parents, tripled between 1994 ($5.1 billion) and 2001 ($18.5 billion).

OPENING UP

CHINA'S ENTRY into the WTO has sparked a fierce American debate over the possible impact on the U.S.-China trade balance. Optimists believe the mainland's participation in the world trade body will stimulate U.S. exports and help narrow America's trade gap with China. Others are far less sanguine, pointing to the removal of global textile restrictions and China's continued unfair trade practices as two major impediments to any gains in trade. Whatever the merits of each position, these arguments fail to see that U.S.-China relations are rapidly being transformed by the investment-driven strategies of multinationals.

At its core, China's WTO accession is about greater access to China's markets and resources. Governments and multilateral institutions brokered that deal. But at the end of the day, firms, not governments, will largely determine the delivery of goods and services to China. In general, U.S. companies view China no differently than they do other foreign markets. That is, they would rather sell their products directly through their foreign affiliates than export them from the United States. When advantages such as cheap labor and a large internal market are present in a host nation, U.S. companies are all too willing to exploit these endowments.

China's massive consumer and labor markets do set it apart from the rest of the world. So for many American firms, there is no choice but to be on the ground. Eastman Kodak, for instance, cannot compete at arm's length from China against its global rival Fuji Photo Film. Nor can Motorola, which confronts an uphill battle there against Nokia, cede the mainland's massive consumer cellular market to the Finnish cell-phone giant. General Motors similarly requires an in-country presence if it hopes to chip away at Volkswagen's leading market position. Even though Chinese tariffs on foreign automobiles are expected to be lowered over the next few years, it is highly unlikely that GM will opt to serve Chinese consumers from afar, through trade, rather than nearby, through investment. For IBM and Compaq, stiff local competition requires a local presence if they are to have any chance of surviving in a highly competitive Chinese market.

For these companies and many others, China's WTO accession represents a green light not so much to trade but to invest, and to enhance existing ties with their foreign affiliates or create new ones. The price of admission into the WTO—lower tariffs, the elimination of numerous nontariff barriers, industry deregulation, and improved intellectual property rights—will allow U.S. parents and affiliates to become even more integrated. Lower tariffs will allow both parties to exchange materials, parts, and finished goods on a more cost-effective basis. The once-simple integration strategies of firms, centered on the processing or assembling of manufactured goods, will become more complex as value-added manufacturing functions are increasingly transferred to Chinese affiliates. The latter will become more specialized as they are brought into the global production networks of the parents. As a result, the quality of affiliate production will rise and become more internationally competitive.

Furthermore, affiliate output for both the local market and for exports will become more interchangeable, promoting increased related-party trade of U.S. exports and imports and greater trade flows in general. And expanded in-country distribution rights will give affiliates better access to the Chinese consumer. The upshot is that the key trends of the late 1990s—increased reliance on foreign affiliate sales as the primary way to deliver goods, and greater use of China as an export platform—will accelerate in the years ahead.

This change will not happen over night. There will be hiccups and hang-ups. But short-term setbacks should not obscure the fact that the two nations are entering a new phase. American firms have already begun to upgrade their investment base in China, as seen in the expanding research and development presence of such technology leaders as Cisco, Microsoft, and Intel. These firms are driving deeper into China to adapt their technology to the local market and tap the potential of China's low-cost but well-educated work force. For the same reasons, world technology leaders such as Advanced Micro Devices, Matsushita, Amkor, and Philips Semiconductor have also made major investments in the mainland. In the end, although everyone agrees that Beijing's entry into the WTO entails deeper U.S.-China links, few realize how these ties will materialize.

"MADE IN CHINA"

OVERCOMING a U.S. trade deficit in excess of $80 billion is not going to be easy if more American firms are using the mainland as a low-cost export base. But the task will be made even tougher by the fact that U.S. firms are not the only ones exporting goods from the mainland. Asia's developing economies have been deploying this strategy for years. European and Japanese multinationals are also rapidly expanding their outsourcing capabilities in China. Indeed, Beijing's WTO accession has only enhanced China's role as the world's preeminent low-cost factory.

One of the most overlooked aspects of the U.S.-China trade relationship is the large percentage of U.S. imports from the mainland produced by foreign enterprises operating there. Cell phones, televisions, video cameras, and printers are typical imports from China—but they are purchased from firms headquartered outside China. Most of the profits from these sales accrue to the parent company, even though these goods, and many others like them, bear the familiar "Made in China" label.

The paucity of data makes it hard to compare U.S. imports from indigenous Chinese firms with imports from foreign enterprises and affiliates. But it is clear that the contribution of foreign enterprises to China's export ascendancy is staggering. From a share of less than two percent in 1985, aggregate exports of foreign-invested enterprises accounted for nearly half of China's total exports in 2000. Affiliate exports from China in 2000— nearly $120 billion—were double Brazil's exports in the same year and exceeded total exports from central Europe. It was export-oriented investment from Hong Kong, Singapore, Taiwan, and South Korea that helped transform China from an producer of primary commodities in the early 1980s into one of the world's leading exporters of light manufactured goods in less than a decade. To offset rising costs at home and exploit China's rock-bottom labor costs, manufacturers of footwear, toys, garments, sporting goods, and other consumer items began to decamp from their own markets for the mainland in the late 1980s. Most of the production in China was for export, which had the effect of boosting America's trade deficit with China while lowering America's deficit with Hong Kong, South Korea, and Taiwan.

In the 1990s, a similar pattern occurred as the world's leading technology firms also migrated to China, shifting the composition of investment from low-end goods to information technology. Once again, China's exports reflected that change. As a share of China's total exports, office machines and telecommunications equipment leapt from a virtually nonexistent share in 1990 to 17.4 percent by 2000. Exports in that category surged by 44 percent in 2000 alone, totaling $43.5 billion and vaulting China into the global high-tech big leagues. The mainland has now become a leading global exporter of machinery and transportation equipment, boosted by annual export growth of 23 percent over the 1990s. China's share of the world's manufactured exports more than doubled again in the last decade, rising from 1.9 percent in 1990 to 4.7 percent in 2000.

China now ranks as the world's sixth-largest exporter of manufactured goods. It could even overtake Japan, which had a global share of 9.7 percent in 2000, as more Japanese firms turn to China as a low-cost export platform. Although Japanese investment flows to China have blown hot and cold over the past decade, China's accession into the WTO and Japan's ongoing recession pushed Japan's investment in China to a record high in 2001. Japan's corporate elite is raising its investment stakes in China, where wages are one-tenth of those in Japan. This change could shift more of Japan's trade deficit with the United States onto the shoulders of China.

COMPETITOR OR PARTNER?

AMERICA'S trade deficit with China is here to stay. But the perennial trade gap need not be a poisonous thorn in the side of both parties if new analytical tools are used to understand and measure the commercial linkages between the United States and China. Trade statistics were useful measurements in the 1980s, when U.S.-China relations represented nothing more than the simple two-way exchange of goods. But today, bilateral links are much more complex, shaped increasingly by foreign investment and the global strategies of multinationals.

Against this backdrop, it is time for one of the best-kept secrets in Washington to be boldly broadcast: American firms deliver their products to foreign customers through not only exports but foreign-affiliate sales. An increase in the ratio of U.S. affiliate sales to exports, as in the case of China, indicates deepening commercial linkages. This variable, not the trade deficit, should be what shapes and influences U.S. economic policy toward China. A single-minded obsession with trade is a recipe for misguided policies.

With this fact in mind, the Bush administration must allocate more resources for the accurate and timely collection of foreign-affiliate data. Last March, the BEA finally released such data for 1999—an unacceptable lag that keeps policymakers in the dark and makes earlier-released trade figures, by default, the official scorecard of U.S.-China commerce. The administration also needs to take the lead in articulating to Congress how firms' strategies influence bilateral trade flows and how a corporate presence in China can positively affect U.S. corporate profits, exports, and jobs. In addition, many in Washington need to understand that although China's trade surplus with the United States is relatively large, a portion of the surplus is recycled back to the United States. China alone accounted for roughly 10 percent of net foreign purchases of U.S. securities last year. In other words, if the United States should opt to curtail commercial links with the mainland, it may be effectively cutting off a key source of foreign capital—something the world's largest debtor nation can hardly afford. For their part, senior managers of corporate America should better explain to the public how their companies compete in one of the most promising yet competitive markets in the world. An interagency committee should be formed to debate and discuss these issues, with subsequent consultations with the Chinese.

These endeavors are not arduous or expensive, but they would pay huge dividends. Rethinking U.S.-China engagement would set the stage for a more informed dialogue with Beijing as China phases in various WTO commitments. It would promote greater cooperation and a spirit of trust between the two parties. Less controversy over trade would help promote a new global trade round and minimize bilateral disputes. It would also provide a more constructive backdrop for other thorny issues between the United States and China.

U.S.-China trade relations have progressed rapidly in the past few years. Future prospects, boosted by China's entry into the WTO, are quite promising. But the bilateral relationship will never reach its full potential as long as policymakers continue to interpret America's large trade deficit with China as a loss of global competitiveness or a result of unfair trade practices. The greatest danger on the U.S.-China trade front is that while many in Washington view China as a "strategic competitor," American businesses have increasingly embraced the mainland as a "strategic partner." This divergence represents a dangerous disconnect that must be reconciled in short order. ☯

China's Coming Transformation

George Gilboy and Eric Heginbotham

THE MAIN EVENT

SOCIAL FORCES unleashed by China's economic reform over the last 20 years are now driving inexorably toward a fundamental transformation of Chinese politics. Since the suppression of the 1989 student protests in Tiananmen Square, China's leaders have struggled to maintain the political status quo, even while pursuing rapid economic reform. The result today is a nonadaptive, brittle state that is unable to cope with an increasingly organized, complex, and robust society. Further efforts to resist political change will only squander the benefits of social and economic dynamism, perpetuate the government's costly battle to contain the populace, drive politics toward increasingly tense domestic confrontation, and ultimately threaten the system with collapse

Many of today's senior Chinese officials recognize this dilemma but have powerful personal motivations to resist change. The next generation of Chinese leaders, however—set to take office in 2002–3—is both more supportive of reform and less constrained by Tiananmen-era political baggage. These new leaders will likely respond to the dilemma, therefore, by accelerating political liberalization.

GEORGE GILBOY and ERIC HEGINBOTHAM are Ph.D. candidates in political science at the Massachusetts Institute of Technology. Gilboy studies industrial technology development and economic institutions in China. Heginbotham studies Chinese civil-military relations and grand strategy. Both have lived in China for more than five years.

This does not imply that China will soon become a Western-style democracy. Rather, the coming steps in reform will likely include measures to legitimize independent social organization, give citizen groups increased input in policymaking (in exchange for some limits on their activities), and develop greater intraparty democracy. These changes will be difficult, and in the near term, they are as likely to throw China into domestic turmoil as they are to create a stable partial democracy.

This coming political reformation is *the* main event in China, and it has critical implications for Sino-U.S. relations. Events such as the recent collision of a U.S. spy plane with a Chinese fighter jet near Hainan Island, the detention of foreign academics in China, or even rhetorical skirmishes across the Taiwan Strait cannot by themselves derail or even significantly delay the forces of change. The event most likely to disrupt the coming reform effort would be the emergence of a clearly adversarial relationship between the United States and China— a new cold war. Such a development would reinforce the position of Chinese conservatives and militarists and weaken the forces that are currently driving change. Accordingly, U.S. policy should be restrained and carefully calibrated to maintain regional security while encouraging continued reform and liberalization in China.

BRITTLE STATE

CHINA'S CURRENT LEADERS view politics through the prism of two central episodes in their political lives: the Cultural Revolution of the mid-1960s and the 1989 Tiananmen Square demonstrations. The Cultural Revolution made today's leaders averse to radicalism and mass action, and the Tiananmen demonstrations made them wary of social and political liberalization. These two experiences have framed the boundaries of "safe" and "stable" politics in China—not too radical, not too liberal.

In the days leading up to the Tiananmen crackdown, the Communist Party's senior leaders came to believe that the demonstrations, if left unchecked, could lead to the violent overthrow of party rule and the onset of social chaos. Firmly implanted in their minds was China's vivid history of small gatherings growing into large movements, often followed by violence and unrest. To these leaders, the Tiananmen demonstrations confirmed that limited political dissent could rapidly attract support from other groups seeking to vent their own dissatisfactions. Indeed, the student gatherings in 1989 began not as protests but as spontaneous mourning for the death of the relatively liberal party leader Hu Yaobang. Once gathered, however, the students quickly added calls for accelerated economic and political reform. Senior party leaders were caught off-guard by the students' vehement criticism and swift organization. They were even more alarmed by the other groups that coalesced in support of the students, especially well-organized urban workers. After weeks of demonstrations and fruitless negotiations, the protesters were finally dispersed by the military, at the cost of many lives.

In the years since, China's leaders have shown little tolerance for challenges to their authority. Although Western headlines tend to focus on Beijing's tough stance against public protests, even more important for China's future may be the regime's general intolerance of independent social organization. The government has not permitted the rise of representative institutions capable of giving people a feeling of participation or investment in the governing system. This unwillingness to deal with groups that are not dominated and controlled by the party locks the state in a constant struggle to hold back a rising tide of self-organizing social and economic entities.

The political rigidity of the current regime stands out when compared to the flexibility of Deng Xiaoping's 1980s leadership. Before 1989, Deng had promoted intraparty democratization, village elections, and the devolution of power to the provinces. He had even promoted the separation of party and state to reduce the Communist Party's interference in administrative affairs. In contrast, the current generation of leaders, including President Jiang Zemin, has eschewed further political and institutional reform in favor of accelerating economic reform.

Despite the current regime's unwillingness to move forward on political reform, Chinese politics and society have remained more stable than most foreign observers predicted in the aftermath of Tiananmen. Since the 1989 uprising, no political dissident movements have been able to inspire similar widespread public support. This quiescence is not simply attributable to the coercion and suppression of civil society. Over the last ten years, Beijing has sustained its non-adaptive state by scoring a series of economic and social successes that have appreciably improved the quality of life for most Chinese.

The most important of these achievements has been increased material prosperity. According to official statistics, China's annual real GDP growth averaged 9.7 percent between 1989 and 2000. In aggregate terms, real urban incomes more than doubled over the same period. For many Chinese families, the increased prosperity of the 1990s can be measured by the new range of goods that they can now afford. The prizes of the 1980s included basic items such as refrigerators and television sets. Today, many Chinese families find computers, designer clothes, mobile phones, and home-entertainment centers within their reach as well.

This growing prosperity is the result of the Chinese government's commitment to structural economic reforms. Measures to legitimize private capital and grant private firms the same legal rights as state-owned businesses have laid the foundation for sustained, market-based growth. Today, more than 40 percent of industrial output comes from private companies, and more than 30 percent of nonagricultural employees work for private or mixed-ownership firms. (In contrast, virtually no privately owned industrial firms existed in 1979 when Deng's economic reform began.)

Beijing has also achieved greater integration with the global economy. China's international trade has more than quadrupled, from $112 billion in 1989 to $474 billion in 2000, and no other country in the world, besides the United States, receives more foreign direct investment. Between 1996 and 1999, China's FDI totaled $126 billion—more than six times that of Japan. Beijing's commitment to join the World Trade Organization (WTO) will further open the economy to foreign trade, investment, and international supervision.

Along with these economic reforms have come greatly expanded personal liberties. Individual Chinese, especially city-dwellers, are now free to create their own lifestyles: they can move about the country, start their own businesses, and express themselves on a wide range of issues. Those who wish to travel abroad can now obtain passports to do so, provided they have enough money. Even China's controversial one-child policy, often a target of criticism in the West, has been relaxed, first in rural communities and more recently in Shanghai.

Jiang's regime has been able to achieve all this while delivering what has been perhaps the most stable decade in the last 150 years of China's tumultuous history. This stability taps into a deep-seated longing among many Chinese to leave behind the misery of past foreign invasions, civil wars, and violent mass political movements. Not only has it provided an environment conducive to economic growth, but it has made most people feel secure that today's new-found wealth can be enjoyed tomorrow.

These achievements have offered both the means and the incentive for new groups to form and organize. But the Chinese leadership, fearful of political dissent and social organization, has been unwilling to adapt politics to new social realities. This reluctance has resulted in a brittle state that is increasingly unable to sustain the social stability and economic growth of the past decade.

ROBUST SOCIETY

ARMED WITH greater wealth and liberty, Chinese society has gained a spirited life of its own, generating a constant stream of both formal and informal organizations. Most of this activity—from labor movements to consumer advocacy to animal-rights activism—is normal and healthy in any market-based economy. But when social dynamism is suppressed, some of its energy is chan-neled into unhealthy activities, such as violent protest. All of this requires the state to find new ways to understand, mediate between, and govern groups in society. One thing is certain: the regime's current methods of social control will not work.

The state's ability to control and coerce the populace has withered. For example, urban neighborhood committees, one of the regime's key means of monitoring its citizens, have dramatically declined in power and relevance. These committees once dominated life in the pervasive housing tracts run by state-owned companies. Through their connection to the work unit, or *danwei,* they ruled over critical aspects of everyday life, such as housing, employment, and benefits, controlling society at the neighborhood level. But over the past two decades of economic reform, rising incomes, a growing private sector, the contraction of state firms, and the privatization of housing have all conspired to weaken the neighborhood committee system. In the countryside, the decline of collective farming has led to a similar relaxation of state control over the lives of individuals.

A fundamental shift in the balance of power between Chinese state and society is underway. With each passing day, the government understands less about its own people, while its power to affect social outcomes wanes. Meanwhile, the number of "actively dissatisfied" groups has grown. In 1989, political dissent was largely limited to activist students, a few reform politicians, and some urban workers. Today, however, new powerful actors have emerged to press for their own interests.

Farmers. With increasing frequency, Chinese farmers are organizing to protest corrupt local officials, onerous and arbitrary taxes, and extreme poverty. In recent months, farmers have attacked tax collectors, blocked roads, and fought with officials and police. In April 2001, for example, more than 600 police and paramilitary troops stormed the southern village of Yuntang, where villagers had barricaded the only road into town and steadfastly refused to pay taxes that they called illegal and unreasonably high.

The unemployed. As economic reform continues, millions of Chinese workers are being laid off each year with little hope of reemployment or adequate social welfare support. In some cities, unemployed workers are now joining together in large-scale protests, involving as many as 20,000 people at a time. Such demonstrations wracked the northeastern cities of Huludao and Liaoyang in the spring of last year. And similar disturbances now occur almost daily in cities and towns throughout the country.

Consumers. Today's Chinese consumers frequently speak out and organize against defective products, financial scams, and official corruption. When these actions are aimed at state agencies or firms, they highlight the government's conflicts of interest as well as the weakness of economic and regulatory institutions. Consumer dissatisfaction may soon become more apparent in China's ill-regulated domestic stock market, in which the government has been encouraging individual investment. Most Chinese investors interpret this encouragement as government assurance that they will make money, and they are likely to hold the government, not the market, responsible for any major shakeout.

Industry associations. Because China's official industry associations are weak and dominated by the Communist Party, they are unable to mediate effectively between industry and government. Yet some industry leaders have coalesced to force the central government to change policies on taxes, international trade, and price reforms. Still, these groups are neither formal nor transparent to the rest of society. They do not fully represent the collective interests of their sectors, nor are they held accountable for their activities. Private entrepreneurs and even state-enterprise managers are now pressuring the government to grant greater independence to official industry associations or to formally recognize unofficial ones. Ironically, working with democratic, independent industry groups is not unknown in China. The central government (and many local governments) already regularly meet with chambers of commerce and industry associations that represent foreign firms in China, often consulting them on key regulatory and policy issues.

Labor unions. Although China's official labor unions, like its formal industry associations, are dominated by the Communist Party, many of them are now pressing for greater organizational independence. And despite the arrests of many would-be organizers of unofficial unions, attempts to establish new, fully independent labor groups continue. Even foreign firms in China have asked the government to allow the formation of stronger, more representative unions because they believe such groups will help their managers better negotiate with their workers.

Religious and spiritual movements. The rise of the Falun Gong is only the most visible indication of resurgent spiritualism in China. Traditional religions, mystical movements, and cults have attracted millions of followers in recent years. Some observers estimate that 30 million Christians now live in China, about half of them belonging to underground churches. In Beijing alone, the number of unauthorized churches has reportedly grown from 200 in 1996 to around 1,000 today. Despite a recent government crackdown that destroyed hundreds of unsanctioned churches and temples, the state will be hard pressed to keep up with today's ever-quickening pace of spiritual activity.

Special-interest groups. A variety of nascent special-interest groups, ranging from environmental and animal-rights organizations to regional soccer clubs (which are sometimes prone to hooliganism), now place new demands on the state for resources and attention. For example, environmental groups—some with nationwide reach—have sponsored direct actions such as tree-planting programs and petitions calling for better municipal waste management. Such groups provide important services to society, but their potential for mobilizing people on a regional or even nationwide scale makes the government nervous.

Separatists. Finally, separatist groups continue to challenge the regime's authority directly. Tibetans have long resisted Chinese rule, sometimes with peaceful protest, sometimes with violence. Muslim separatists in the westernmost province of Xinjiang receive training and weapons from Muslim groups in Central Asia and are engaged in armed confrontation with the state. Their most militant elements attack police, soldiers, and other government officials, and the state has responded with equal force. According to estimates from international observers, 210 people were sentenced to death for separatist activities between 1997 and 1999.

It is becoming difficult for the Chinese government to ignore or conceal these social changes. Information on even the most sensitive topics is available from foreign sources across increasingly porous borders, and even China's state-run media have become a regular source of news on many domestic problems. As a result, nearly everyone in China today is aware of the beneficial work of entrepreneurs, consumer groups, and animal-rights activists. They also receive detailed reports about railroad disruptions and factory seizures by disgruntled workers, as well as pervasive corruption among village officials. Increased access to information has helped create a public opinion in China, and the regime already feels obliged to respond.

RISING TO THE CHALLENGE

COPING WITH China's increasingly organized and informed society is the greatest challenge facing Beijing's next generation of leaders.

The nation's new leaders will seek ways not only to maintain continued economic growth but also to reinvigorate legitimacy and popular support. A key element of this reformation will be greater acceptance of and dialogue with legitimate independent associations. Both state and society would benefit from the success of such efforts. The state would be better able to govern, and society would enjoy greater pluralism and new limits on state intervention.

China's new leaders will likely choose change over retrenchment for three reasons. First, many senior officials already recognize that the task of confronting society is becoming more burdensome and difficult. The stability of the last decade is showing signs of wearing thin. According to a speech attributed to Prime Minister Zhu Rongji, China suffered 117 incidents of armed, violent protest last year. Those incidents resulted in more than 4,300 casualties, of which more than half were party cadres and government officials. In some of these cases, thousands of security personnel were mobilized before order was restored.

Although these protests have not yet reached the size and significance of the 1989 Tiananmen demonstrations, they have been enough to lead some party officials to question Beijing's current inflexibility on social and political issues. For example, several senior provincial police cadres—overwhelmed by their duties to contain the Falun Gong—have reportedly petitioned the leadership to take a more accommodating approach toward the spiritual group. For some business managers, many of whom are also party members, the crackdown and its associated political study sessions have diverted attention from pressing administrative, commercial, and management problems. Indeed, dissent within the party on the Falun Gong issue may run deep: even some top officials may believe that the government's policy has gone too far.

A second incentive for political reform is that the continued suppression of social organization and institution building threatens to hamper economic development. Weak institutions contribute to waste and inefficiency, discourage investment, and limit the prospects for further rapid growth. Foreign firms in China have long complained about the lack of market information, clear regulations, enforceable contracts, and good coordination among suppliers. The costs of these inadequacies are also high for Chinese companies. Weak economic institutions—such as the party-dominated labor unions and industry associations—cannot effectively exchange people and information, pool resources, set standards, present policymakers with unified industry views, or even adequately interact with one another. These shortcomings result in fragmented industries, isolated firms, and poorly informed managers, all of which raise costs and discourage investment in new, productive businesses.

The weakness of economic institutions also threatens to retard the technological learning and innovation that is critical for future productivity gains and economic growth. Innovation is not simply a matter of money, science, or market competition—although all three elements are essential. Innovation also requires close interaction among firms, universities, research and development institutes, and all levels of government. In many of the world's most innovative countries, this interaction often occurs through regional development agencies, industry and professional associations, and sector-specific financial consortia. Yet in China, despite appeals by industrial leaders and even state science and technology officials, the regime's reluctance to accept independent civil society has stifled the development of such organizations. Beijing's Zhongguancun area—often called China's Silicon Valley—has generated little real innovation, largely because it lacks the dense interfirm networks and cooperative business culture that has made America's Silicon Valley so successful.

The third reason that China's new leaders will likely choose change stems from their personal affiliations and career interests. The clear front-runner to replace Jiang is Vice President Hu Jintao, whose political background is in the Communist Youth League, a relatively liberal wing of the party. Even though Hu may not emerge as the primary driver of political reform (and indeed may take a relatively cautious position on that issue), he will likely try to promote an unprecedented number of officials with Youth League and other reform-related backgrounds. This drive may be complemented by the efforts of today's reform-minded leaders (such as Zhu Rongji and Li Ruihuan) to promote their own protégés.

Regardless of who gains which specific posts in the government, powerful political motivations may also drive the new leadership toward reform. In the decade since the Tiananmen Square crisis, many hard-line leaders have passed from the scene, and those that remain have become more vulnerable to major revisions of the verdict on that issue. Accordingly, those untainted by the legacy of Tiananmen are increasingly tempted to leapfrog over their seniors by seizing the banner of reform. This trend has already begun, with the disclosure of the *Tiananmen Papers* and other documents now being smuggled out of China by factions of the Communist Party.

CONTAINING CHINA'S REFORM?

FOR CHINA'S next generation of leaders, political reform will center on allowing independent social organizations to formally represent their interests, strengthening intraparty democracy, and increasing the separation of the Communist Party from the state. These measures will recast relations between state and society and could be the first steps toward greater political pluralism. The experiences of South Korea, Mexico, and Taiwan demonstrate that a variety of paths can lead from one-party rule toward political liberalization. None of them offers a quick and painless transition to full democracy. Rather, they entail a gradual conciliation with society's new forces and a phased-in introduction of democratic institutions and values.

Nor is success guaranteed. It will be difficult to govern China's huge, powerful, and potentially fractious society during the inevitable disruptions of a major transition. Even if intent on reform, China's new leadership could botch the job. If it does, the China of tomorrow could look more like today's Indonesia or Yugoslavia than South Korea or Taiwan. Whatever the outcome, China is on the cusp of more than just a change in leadership personnel. The coming set of reforms is likely to set in motion a process of political change that may be longer and more tumultuous than anyone has yet imagined. Despite these risks, however, it is in the interest of Beijing's next generation to attempt reform. And it is in the interest of the United States to encourage them to do so.

The advent of a new cold war between the United States and China, however, would discourage Beijing's new leaders from pursuing political reform. Explicitly adversarial Sino-U.S. relations would validate Chinese conservatives' arguments about American intentions to weaken China and would leave Chinese liberals open to charges of treason. Moreover, even tomorrow's moderate leaders would be unlikely to run the high risks of reform if they feared the United States might exploit Chinese political divisions. Hence, although the United States needs to defend its legitimate interests in East Asia, it should do so in a restrained manner that provides the least ammunition for reactionary critics in China. In short, Washington should avoid a containment policy that would actually contain China's reform process.

Although dramatic change may still be several years away, moderation and restraint in U.S. policy are needed now. Today's reform-minded leaders are struggling to promote their protégés to key positions in preparation for the coming political transition. The next generation, which will govern China until at least 2008, is still being forged, and specific personnel selections will have a decisive impact on the prospects for reform. It will be difficult, however, for relatively liberal officials to rise to key positions if Sino-U.S. relations descend into cold war.

The United States can take steps to avoid increasing tensions without compromising its core interests. One of the least costly— and most effective—measures is rhetorical moderation. Although suggesting that China could become a "strategic partner" (as the Clinton administration did) was premature but benign, labeling China a "strategic competitor" (as some in the current administration have done) is both premature and pernicious.

The United States should also focus greater attention on the strategic and diplomatic implications of its tactical military activities. Although the U.S. military presence in East Asia generally enhances regional stability, some types of military activities can have adverse effects. China's handling of the recent spy-plane crash near Hainan angered most Americans. Yet American surveillance close to Chinese borders had been conducted at a Cold War level of intensity for a year before the incident occurred. Such U.S.

activities may not violate international law, but the intensity and manner in which they have been conducted recently has created an image of a hostile United States without commensurate gains for American security interests.

Indeed, a more measured approach to secondary security interests would enhance U.S. leverage on more vital issues, such as halting the proliferation of missiles and weapons of mass destruction (WMD) and encouraging a peaceful resolution of the standoff across the Taiwan Strait. Confrontation could convince China's leaders that WMD proliferation is in their national interest, whereas a firm but more businesslike relationship would help persuade them that it is not. By focusing on core issues, America's voice on them will be amplified.

Chinese civilian leaders, especially those about to take the helm in 2002–3, do not want a new cold war. Confrontation with the United States would jeopardize China's economic reform program and continued prosperity. A cold war would also diminish the civilian leadership's authority relative to that of the military. Having struggled for 20 years to curb the army's role in domestic policy, civilian leaders would be loath to invite the resurgence of military influence that would accompany a descent into cold war.

Moreover, the civilian leadership's ability to use confrontation with the United States to gain popular support for the party is severely limited. Beijing does use historical education to promote the ideas of national unity and past victimization. The government has also permitted the limited expression of social anger immediately following events such as the accidental U.S. bombing of the Chinese embassy in Belgrade. But in all such cases officials have moved quickly to contain domestic passions for fear that even nationalist movements may ultimately threaten the regime itself.

Change is the main event in China, and America should welcome it. Chinese hard-liners will not be able to stop the coming political reform—unless they are aided by an adversarial attitude from the United States. As a great power, the United States can best serve its own interests, as well as those of the Asian region, by behaving with the restraint and grace befitting its status.

China's "War on Terror"

September 11 and Uighur Separatism

Chien-peng Chung

IN THE WAKE OF THE SEPTEMBER 11 attacks on the United States, China has launched its own "war on terror." Beijing now labels as terrorists those who are fighting for an independent state in the northwestern province of Xinjiang, which the separatists call "Eastern Turkestan." The government considers these activists part of a network of international Islamic terror, with funding from the Middle East, training in Pakistan, and combat experience in Chechnya and Afghanistan.

In fact, separatist violence in Xinjiang is neither new nor driven primarily by outsiders. The region's Uighurs, most of whom practice Sufi Islam and speak a Turkic language, have long had their national ambitions frustrated by Beijing. The latest wave of Uighur separatism has been inspired not by Osama bin Laden but by the unraveling of the Soviet Union, as militants seek to emulate the independence gained by some Muslim communities in Central Asia. For a decade now, Xinjiang has been rocked by demonstrations, bombings, and political assassinations. According to a recent government report, Uighur separatists were responsible for 200 attacks between 1990 and 2001, causing 162 deaths and injuring more than 440 people. In the largest single incident, in 1997, as many as 100 people may have been killed during a pro-independence uprising in the town of Ili, with the government and the separatists blaming each other for the fatalities. These incidents have occurred despite the best efforts of the

CHIEN-PENG CHUNG is Assistant Professor at the Institute of Defence and Strategic Studies in Singapore.

Chinese authorities to suppress them. As part of their continuing "strike hard" campaign against crime, for example, Chinese police recently reported the arrest of 166 separatist "terrorists" and other "major criminals" in a series of raids carried out in Urumqi, Xinjiang's capital.

The separatists have accused the regime of resorting to arbitrary arrest, torture, detention without public trial, and summary execution. The Chinese government, meanwhile, has alleged that members of a shadowy "Eastern Turkestan Islamic Movement" have obtained funds and training from al Qaeda. As the security environment in Xinjiang grows increasingly tense, the conflict shows just how complicated such struggles can be, and how inadequate purely repressive approaches are in dealing with them.

BEG TO DIFFER

CHINA'S QING DYNASTY completed its annexation of what is now Xinjiang in 1759, and the region's first demand for independence can be traced to an uprising by a local chieftain named Yakub Beg in 1865. He fought fierce battles against the armies of the Chinese court and even managed to secure, in return for trade concessions, diplomatic recognition from tsarist Russia and the United Kingdom. Although finally defeated in 1877, Beg's campaign set a precedent by calling for Uighur independence based on appeals to religion and ethnicity.

With the end of China's imperial era, the Uighurs (in combination with other local Muslim groups) twice briefly achieved statehood. From 1931 to 1934, and again from 1944 to 1949, separate regimes calling themselves the Eastern Turkestan Republic were set up in Xinjiang. The first, which started in the city of Hami, was crushed by a local warlord representing the government of the erstwhile Republic of China. The second, which centered on the districts of Ili, Altai, and Chugachak, was pressured into integrating with the People's Republic of China shortly after the latter's formation. For the next four decades, Xinjiang's Communist rulers kept the lid on ethnic separatism in the region through iron-fisted control. But for many Uighurs the aspiration for a country of their own never went away.

Today the million-strong Uighur émigré community provides support for several separatist political organizations. Located across the globe, these organizations are not all radical; indeed, many do not advocate violence at all. The Washington, D.C.–based Eastern Turkestan National Freedom Center, for instance, lobbies members of Congress on behalf of the Uighur cause and publishes books and tapes on pan-Turkic nationalism for circulation inside Xinjiang. Meanwhile, the leader of the Europe-based Eastern Turkestan Union, Erkin Alptekin, prefers to organize conferences and work with Tibetan émigré groups seeking autonomy for their own homeland. In truth, whether or not they support the use of violent methods, the Xinjiang separatist groups both at home and abroad are too small, dispersed, and faceless to constitute a threat to Chinese control over the region. Beijing fears them nevertheless, because the mere possibility that they may cause disruption creates an impression of social instability in Xinjiang and dampens foreign investment.

The Chinese government has alleged that "more than a thousand" Xinjiang separatists have received terrorist training in Afghanistan and claims to have arrested a hundred foreign-trained terrorists who have made their way back to Xinjiang. But only one Uighur separatist organization, the Eastern Turkestan Islamic Party of Allah, appears conclusively to have operated in Afghanistan. Its identity was exposed when its putative leader, Alerkan Abula, was executed by the Chinese authorities in January 2001. Other groups, such as the East Turkestan Opposition Party, the Revolutionary Front of Eastern Turkestan, the Organization for Turkestan Freedom, and the Organization for the Liberation of Uighurstan, have links to small guerrilla cells based in the oasis towns of Xinjiang's Taklimakan Desert. The guerrillas have raided government laboratories and warehouses for explosive materials and manufactured various types of bombs. The Turkey-based Organization for Turkestan Freedom, for example, claimed responsibility for the bombing of a bus in Beijing on March 7, 1997, injuring 30 people. The Chinese government also suspects this organization of attacks on the Chinese embassy in Ankara and the Chinese consulate in Istanbul that same year.

Despite the separatists' efforts, China is unlikely to relinquish control of the province. With 18 million people, Xinjiang produces one-third of China's cotton, and explorations in the Tarim Basin have revealed the country's largest oil and gas reserves. The region borders Mongolia, Russia, several Central Asian republics, Pakistan, and India, making it a useful springboard for projecting Chinese influence abroad. And Beijing realizes that acquiescing to Uighur demands will only embolden separatists in Tibet and Taiwan.

The government has also invested a great deal in the region. As part of a grand scheme to develop China's western areas, Beijing plans to spend more than 100 billion yuan ($12 billion) on 70 major projects in Xinjiang over the next five years, mostly to improve infrastructure. The government has recently completed a railway linking the remote western city of Kashgar to the rest of Xinjiang. And the regime is considering proposals for using foreign investment to build oil and gas pipelines from Central Asia across the Taklimakan Desert.

DEFINING MOMENT

THE U.S. ACTION in Afghanistan presented a dilemma for the Uighurs. On the streets of Urumqi, Kashgar, and other cities in Xinjiang, opinions both for and against the U.S. antiterrorist effort could be heard. Many Uighurs expressed sympathy for their Taliban friends and fellow Muslims across the border in Afghanistan, who had provided sanctuary, arms, and training to Xinjiang separatist fighters over the years. Yet the Uighurs also had positive feelings toward the United States, which had occasionally spoken out against Beijing's violations of their rights.

The September 11 attacks and the subsequent crisis also created a dilemma for China. They offered an opportunity for the government to reframe its battle with the Uighur separatists as part of a larger international struggle against terrorism. But the Afghan campaign raised other, less comfortable issues as well. As a result the Chinese response to the U.S. war on terror has been muted. China supported two UN Security Council resolutions that condemned global terrorism in general terms, but since then Beijing has remained notably silent, a reflection of its ambivalence.

On the one hand, China sees the U.S. fight against al Qaeda as helping to safeguard the authority and effectiveness of national governments. On the other, it worries about the legal and diplomatic repercussions of sanctioning such a clear violation of state sovereignty as the invasion of Afghanistan. It was fortunate for China that no UN resolution seeking to ratify the legality of the U.S.-led military campaign was introduced. A vote against such a resolution would have been seen by Washington as an unfriendly gesture, but a vote for could have set a precedent legitimizing the sort of intrusive foreign military interventions that China has generally opposed. And abstaining would have made the Chinese government look weak and indecisive in the fight against global terrorism.

The Chinese government has tried to equate America's fight against Osama bin Laden and al Qaeda with its own battle against the separatists of Xinjiang. Beijing is signaling to Washington that it wants a free hand in dealing with what it perceives to be foreign-sponsored terrorists on its soil, just as the United States is doing at home and abroad. The Bush administration, however, has been reluctant to equate the fight against "terrorists with global reach" with domestic crackdowns against separatists in China and elsewhere. Rather, Washington has made it clear to the Chinese that nonviolent separatist activities cannot be classified as terrorism.

The problem is that some of the Xinjiang activists do in fact use violence to achieve their goals. Distinguishing between genuine counterterrorism and the repression of minority rights can thus be difficult, as can be determining which acts of terrorism are "international" and which are purely domestic. Foreign-backed militant separatism, a not uncommon phenomenon of which Uighur activism is an example, poses intellectual and legal problems as well as practical ones. Clear guidelines are needed to determine when political refugees can be extradited or punished for supporting separatism from beyond a country's borders, for example, or when international law justifies the use of force against citizens who receive weapons, funding, and training from abroad. Otherwise, precedents might accumulate suggesting it is acceptable for some governments to go after foreign sources of terrorism, but not for others.

WHITHER THE UIGHURS?

WHAT BEIJING NEEDS to recognize is that its own policies are the root causes of Uighur resentment. Rather than trying to stamp out the problem through force and repression alone, the Chinese government should instead do what it can to improve the conditions that fuel separatist feelings.

The government's call to develop the west has accelerated migration by Han Chinese into Xinjiang, thereby exacerbating tensions. In 1949, the region was almost 90 percent Uighur; today, that figure has dropped to 45–50 percent. Many Uighurs do not speak Mandarin Chinese, which is usually the prerequisite for any good-paying job or government position, and few are as well educated as the immigrants. As a result, the Han dominate commerce in Xinjiang's urban areas and are frequently seen by the locals as having the region's best jobs in the government, the Communist Party, and the military. The Han also usually live in newer neighborhoods and go to informally segregated schools.

Rather than allowing the flow of immigration into Xinjiang to remain unchecked, the Chinese regime should regulate it so that immigrants do not compete unnecessarily with the locals for jobs, schools, or state services. Beijing should encourage public-sector corporations, oil companies, and government agencies to increase their hiring of ethnic minorities. Quotas for Uighur admission into colleges and government positions should also be expanded and enforced. The government must also allocate funds fairly among Han and Uighur neighborhoods. Cleaning up the area around China's nuclear test site at Lop Nor in the Taklimakan Desert, where soil and groundwater pollution are causing birth defects and health problems among the local inhabitants, would be another important step.

Furthermore, as guaranteed in the Chinese constitution, the government must uphold religious freedom. Muslim Uighurs who openly practice their faith complain of harassment by the authorities. The regime must respect Muslim customs and allow the free functioning of mosques and religious schools, interfering only if they are found to be educating or harboring militants. Political changes are required as well: less gerrymandering in favor of Han Chinese among Xinjiang's administrative units, more proportionate ethnic representation in party and government structures, and more devolution of power from Beijing to the region.

Hunting down terrorists is only a partial solution to the violence in Xinjiang. Unless China listens to the Uighurs and treats them better, its troubled western region is unlikely to be calmed any time soon.

China's Governance Crisis

Minxin Pei

MORE THAN MUSICAL CHAIRS

PREDICTING THE OUTCOME of China's upcoming leadership succession has become a popular parlor game in certain Washington circles. The curiosity aroused by the transition is understandable, given the huge stakes involved for the world's largest country. If all goes well, the Chinese Communist Party (CCP) is scheduled to select a new and younger leadership at its Sixteenth Party Congress this fall. The incumbent CCP general secretary, 76-year-old Jiang Zemin, may step down and be replaced by China's Vice President Hu Jintao, who is 59. The all-powerful Politburo Standing Committee will see most of its members retire, as will the important Central Committee. In addition, Chinese Premier Zhu Rongji is to step down in March, and Li Peng, the leader of the National People's Congress (the country's legislature), may be heading for the exit as well.

In a country ruled largely by man, not law, succession creates rare opportunities for political intrigue and policy change. Thus, speculation is rife about the composition, internal rivalries, and policy implications of a post-Jiang leadership. The backgrounds of those expected to ascend to the top unfortunately reveal little. By and large, the majority of new faces are technocrats. Some have stellar résumés but thin records; other front-runners boast solid experience as provincial party bosses but carry little national clout.

In any case, conjectures about the immediate policy impact of the pending leadership change are an exercise in futility, because

MINXIN PEI, Senior Associate at the Carnegie Endowment for International Peace, is completing a book titled *China's Trapped Transition: The Limits of Developmental Autocracy.*

Jiang will likely wield considerable influence even after his semi-retirement. A truly dominant new leader may not emerge in Beijing for another three to five years. And regardless of the drama that the succession process might provide, a single-minded focus on power plays in Beijing misses the real story: China is facing a hidden crisis of governance. This fact ought to preoccupy those who believe that much more is at stake in Beijing than a game of musical chairs.

The idea of an impending governance crisis in Beijing may sound unduly alarmist. To the outside world, China is a picture of dynamism and promise. Its potential market size, consistently high growth rates, and recent accession to the World Trade Organization have made the Middle Kingdom a top destination of foreign direct investment ($46 billion in 2001), and multinational corporations salivate at the thought of its future growth. But beneath this giddy image of progress and prosperity lies a different reality—one that is concealed by the glitzy skylines of Shanghai, Beijing, and other coastal cities. The future of China, and the West's interests there, depends critically on how Beijing's new leaders deal with this somber reality.

DOT COMMUNISM AND ITS DISCONTENTS

CHINA'S CURRENT CRISIS results from fundamental contradictions in the reforms that it has pursued over the past two decades—a period that has seen the amazing transformation of the communist regime from one that was infatuated with class struggle to one obsessed by growth rates. This "dot communism," characterized by the marriage of a Leninist party to bureaucratic capitalism with a globalist gloss, has merely disguised, rather than eliminated, these contradictions. But they are growing ever harder to ignore. The previously hidden costs of transition have begun to surface: Further change implies not simply a deepening of market liberalization but also the implementation of political reforms that could endanger the CCP's monopoly on power.

These emerging contradictions are embedded in the very nature of the Chinese regime. For example, the government's market-oriented economic policies, pursued in a context of autocratic and predatory politics, make the CCP look like a self-serving, capitalistic ruling elite, and not a "proletarian party" championing the interests of working people. The party's professed determination to maintain political supremacy also runs counter to its declared goals of developing a "socialist market economy" and "ruling the country according to law," because the minimum requirements of a market economy and the rule of law are institutionalized curbs on political power. The CCP's ambition to modernize Chinese society leaves unanswered the question of how increasing social autonomy will be protected from government caprice. And the party's perennial fear of independently organized interest groups does not prepare it for the inevitable emergence of such groups in an industrialized economy. These unresolved contradictions, inherent in the country's transition away from communism, are the source of rising tensions in China's polity, economy, and society.

During the go-go 1990s, the irreconcilable nature of these contradictions was obscured by rising prosperity and relative political tranquility. Economically, accelerating liberalization and deepening integration with the world marketplace produced unprecedented prosperity, even though some tough reforms (especially those affecting the financial sector and state-owned enterprises, or SOEs) lagged behind. Politically, the ruling elite drew its own lesson from the collapse of Soviet communism ("It's the economy, stupid") and closed ranks behind a strategy that prioritized economic growth and left the political system untouched.

HU JINTAO

This strategy worked for a decade. Within the regime, conservatives who opposed market reforms were marginalized. China's pro-democracy movement, which peaked with the Tiananmen Square protest in 1989, also waned after its leadership was decapitated through exile or imprisonment. The resulting tranquility ended the polarized debate between liberals and conservatives of the 1980s. But ironically, this shift also silenced those at both ends of the ideological spectrum who would have cried that the emperor had no clothes. Thus, the regime escaped pressure to adopt deeper political reforms to relieve the tensions produced by the contradictions of dot communism. With rising wealth and loose talk of a "China century," even some skeptics thought the CCP had managed to square the circle.

The incompatibilities between China's current political system, however, and the essential requirements of the rule of law, a market economy, and an open society have not been washed away by waves of foreign investment. Pragmatists might view these contradictions as inconsequential cognitive nuisances. Unfortunately, their effects are real: they foreclose reform options that otherwise could be adopted for the regime's own long-term good. To be sure, China's pragmatic leaders have made a series of tactical adjustments to weather many new socioeconomic challenges, such as the CCP's recent outreach to entrepreneurs. But these moves are no substitute for genuine institutional reforms that would reinvigorate and relegitimize the ruling party.

THE BUBBLE BURSTS

IN RETROSPECT, the 1990s ought to be viewed as a decade of missed opportunities. The CCP leadership could have taken advantage of a booming economy to renew itself through a program of gradual political reform built on the rudimentary steps of the 1980s. But it did not, and now the cumulative costs of a decade of foot-dragging are becoming more visible. In many crucial respects, China's hybrid neo-authoritarian order eerily exhibits the pathologies of both the political stagnation of Leonid Brezhnev's Soviet Union and the crony capitalism of Suharto's Indonesia.

These pathologies—such as pervasive corruption, a collusive local officialdom, elite cynicism, and mass disenchantment—are the classic symptoms of degenerating governing capacity. In most political systems, a regime's capacity to govern is measured by how it performs three key tasks: mobilizing political support, providing public goods, and managing internal tensions. These three functions of governance—legitimation, performance, and conflict resolution—are, in reality, intertwined. A regime capable of providing adequate public goods (education, public health, law and order) is more likely to gain popular support and keep internal tensions low. In a Leninist party-state however, effective governance critically hinges on the health of the ruling party. Strong organizational discipline, accountability, and a set of core values with broad appeal are essential to governing effectively. Deterioration of the ruling party's strength, on the other hand, sets in motion a downward cycle that can severely impair the party-state's capacity to govern.

Numerous signs within China indicate that precisely such a process is producing huge governance deficits. The resulting strains are making the political and economic choices of China's rulers increasingly untenable. They may soon be forced to undertake risky reforms to stop the rot. If they do not, dot communism could be no more durable than the dot coms.

THE PARTY'S OVER

THE DECLINE of the CCP began during the rule of Mao Zedong, as the late leader's political radicalism, culminating in the madness of the Cultural Revolution (1966–76), deeply damaged the ruling party. The ascent of Deng Xiaoping and his progressive reforms slowed this process, as economic gains, the end of mass repression, and the expansion of personal freedoms partially repaired the CCP's tarnished image.

But Deng's pro-market reforms produced a different set of dynamics that began to corrode the CCP's support. As economic reform deepened, large segments of Chinese society became poorer (such as grain-producing farmers and workers in SOEs). The revenue-starved state was unable to compensate these losers from reform. Consequently, the CCP had little means to secure the political support of these disaffected groups beyond exhorting self-sacrifice and making empty promises of better times ahead.

Some members of the ruling elite also converted their political power into economic gains, building and profiting from patronage machines. In one survey, about two-thirds of the officials being trained at a municipal party school said their promotion depended solely on the favors of their superiors; only five percent thought their own efforts could advance their careers. A ruling party fractured from within by such personalized patronage systems is hardly capable of building broad-based support within society.

It is worth noting that mass political campaigns, a previous hallmark of the CCP's prowess, have virtually vanished from the Chinese political scene. An obvious explanation is that such campaigns tend to be disruptive and lead to political excesses, as they did during the Mao years. A more likely cause, however, is that the CCP no longer possesses the political appeal or the organizational capacity required to launch such campaigns even when it desires them (as was the case during Beijing's efforts to contain pro-democracy dissidents in the late 1980s and the Falun Gong spiritual movement in the late 1990s). Increasingly, when faced with direct challenges to its authority, the CCP can rely only on repression rather than public mobilization to counter its opponents.

IMMOBILIZED

THE EXTENT of the CCP's decline can be measured in three areas: the shrinkage of its organizational penetration, the erosion of its authority and appeal among the masses, and the breakdown of its internal discipline. The organizational decline of the CCP is, in retrospect, almost predetermined. Historically, Leninist parties have thrived only in economies dominated by the state. Such an economy provides the economic institutions (SOEs and collective farms) that form the organizational basis for the ruling party. By pursuing market reforms that have eliminated rural communes and most SOEs, the CCP has fallen victim to its own success. The new economic infrastructure, based on household farming, private business, and individual labor mobility, is inhospitable to a large party apparatus. For instance, an internal CCP report characterized half of the party's rural cells as "weak" or "paralyzed" in recent years. In urban areas, the CCP has been unable to penetrate the emerging private sector, while its old organizational base has collapsed along with the SOEs. In 2000, the CCP did not have a single member in 86 percent of the country's 1.5 million private firms and could establish cells in only one percent of private companies.

The CCP's organizational decay is paralleled by the decline of its authority and image among the public. A survey of 818 migrant laborers in Beijing in 1997–98 revealed that the prevailing image of the ruling party was that of a self-serving elite. Only 5 percent of the interviewees thought their local party cadres "work for the interests of the villagers," and 60 percent said their local officials "use their power only for private gains." Other surveys have revealed similar negative public perceptions of the CCP. A 1998 study of 12,000 urban and rural residents across 10 provinces conducted by the CCP's antigraft agency found that only 43 percent of respondents agreed that "the majority of party and government officials are clean," and that fully one-third said "only a minority of party and government officials are clean."

At the same time as public officials are losing respect, the party's ideological appeal has all but evaporated. Polls conducted by the official national trade union in 1996 showed that only 15 percent of the workers surveyed regarded communism as "their highest ideal," while 70 percent said that their top priority was to pursue individual happiness. Even members of the ruling elite are beginning, albeit reluctantly, to admit this reality. A poll conducted in 1998 among 673 CCP officials in the northeastern province of Jilin found that 35 percent thought the status and authority of government officials had declined.

At the heart of the CCP's organizational and reputational decline is the breakdown of its members' ideological beliefs and internal discipline. Cynicism and corruption abound. The sale of government offices by local CCP bosses was unheard of in the 1980s but became widespread in the 1990s. A 1998 survey of 2,000 provincial officials, conducted by the official antigraft agency, found that 45 percent of respondents thought such practices were continuing unabated.

Even more worrying, the CCP appears unable to enforce internal discipline despite the mortal threat posed by corruption, which has surpassed unemployment as the most serious cause of social instability. Recent official actions, especially the prosecution and execution of several senior officials, create the impression that the CCP leadership is committed to combating corruption. But a comprehensive look at the data tells a different story. Most corrupt officials caught in the government's dragnet seem to have gotten off with no more than a slap on the wrist. For example, of the 670,000 party members disciplined for wrongdoing from 1992 to 1997, only 37,500, or six percent, were punished by criminal prosecution. Indeed, self-policing may be impossible for a ruling party accountable to no one. According to a top CCP official, the party has in recent years expelled only about one percent of its members.

Perhaps the greatest contributing factor to the CCP's political decline is, ironically, the absence of competition. Competition would have forced the party to redefine its mission and recruit members with genuine public appeal. But like monopoly firms, the CCP has devoted its energies to preventing the emergence of competition. Without external pressures, monopolies such as the CCP inevitably develop a full range of pathologies such as patronage systems, organizational dystrophy, and unresponsiveness. Moreover, one-party regimes can rarely take on the new competitors that emerge when the political environment changes suddenly. The fall of the Soviet bloc regimes and the defeat of similar monopolistic parties in the developing world (such as Mexico's Institutional Revolutionary Party) show that an eroding capacity for political mobilization poses a long-term threat to the CCP.

FAILING STATE?

IN A PARTY-STATE, the ruling party's weakness unavoidably saps the state's power. Such "state incapacitation," which in its extreme form results in failed states, is exemplified by the government's increasing inability to provide essential services, such as public safety, education, basic health care, environmental protection, and law enforcement. In China, these indices have been slipping over the past two decades. This decline is especially alarming since it has occurred while the Chinese economy has been booming.

Most of the evidence of the government's deteriorating performance is mundane but telling. Take, for example, the number of traffic fatalities (a key measure of a state's capacity to regulate a routine, but vital, social activity: transportation). Chinese roads are almost twice as deadly today as they were in 1985; there were about 58 road fatalities per 10,000 vehicles in 2000, compared to 34 in 1985. An international comparison using 1995 data shows that traffic fatality risks were much higher in China than in India or Indonesia. Indeed, China fared better only than Tonga, Bangladesh, Myanmar, and Mongolia in the Asia-Pacific region.

Although China has made tremendous progress in improving education, its recent performance lags behind that of many developing countries. China's education spending in 1998 was a mere 2.6 percent of GDP, below the average of 3.4 percent for low-income countries. In fact, China spends almost a third less on education than does India. As a result, access to primary and intermediate education is as low as 40 percent among school-age children in the country's poor western regions.

China's public health-care system has decayed considerably in recent years and compares poorly with those of its neighbors. According to the World Health Organization, China's health system ranked 144th worldwide, placing it among the bottom quartile of WHO members, behind India, Indonesia, and Bangladesh. China's agricultural population has been hit especially hard, as government neglect has led to a near-total collapse of the rural public-health infrastructure. According to the 1998 survey conducted by the Ministry of Health, 37 percent of ill farmers did not seek medical treatment because they could not afford it, and 65 percent of sick peasants needing hospitalization were not admitted because they could not pay. Both figures were higher than in 1993, when a similar survey was carried out. Poor health has become the chief cause of poverty in rural China; 40–50 percent of those who fell below the poverty line in 2000 in some provinces did so only after becoming seriously ill. Even more troubling, the crumbling public-health infrastructure is a principal cause of the rapid spread of HIV and AIDS in China. The UN warned in a recent study that "China is on the verge of a catastrophe that could result in unimaginable human suffering, economic loss, and social devastation."

State incapacitation also manifests itself in worsening environmental degradation. This problem poses perhaps the deadliest threat to China's continued economic development. About a third of the country suffers from severe soil erosion, 80 percent of wastewater is discharged untreated, 75 percent of the country's lakes and about half its rivers have been polluted, and nine of the ten cities with the worst air pollution in the world in 1999 were located in China.

China suffers huge direct economic losses from this environmental damage. The World Bank estimated in the mid-1990s that major forms of pollution cost the country 7.7 percent of its GDP. Beyond this measurable cost, environmental degradation, together with the collapse of much of the agricultural infrastructure built before the 1980s, may have exacerbated the effects of natural disasters. Grain losses resulting from natural disasters have more than doubled in the last 50 years, with most of the increase recorded in the 1990s.

BUSTING THE BUDGET

THE CENTRAL CAUSE of the declining effectiveness of the Chinese state is a dysfunctional fiscal system that has severely undercut the government's ability to fund public services while creating ample opportunities for corruption. Government data misleadingly suggest that the state experienced a massive loss of revenue over the last two decades, as its tax receipts fell from 31 percent of GDP in 1978 to 14 percent in 1999. The truth, however, is quite different. Aggregate government revenue over the past 20 years has held steady at about 30 percent of GDP. What has changed is the massive diversion of revenue from the government budget; increasingly, income collected by the government is not listed in the official budget. At their peak in the mid-1990s, such off-budget earnings exceeded budgeted tax revenue by two to one.

Provincial and municipal governments are the primary beneficiaries of this system because it allows them to raise revenue outside the normal tax streams. Because local officials are more likely to get promoted for delivering short-term growth or other such tangible results, off-budget revenue tends to be spent on building local industries and other projects that do little to improve education, health, or the environment. Moreover, since normal budget rules do not apply to such revenue, officials enjoy near-total discretion over its spending. Consequently, corruption is widespread. Large portions of this off-budget money have been found stashed away in secret slush funds controlled by government officials. In 1999, the National Auditing Agency claimed to have uncovered slush funds and illegal expenditures that amounted to 10 percent of 1998's tax revenue.

An important consequence of this dysfunctional fiscal system is the near collapse of local public finance in many counties and townships, particularly in the populous rural interior provinces (such as Henan, Anhui, and Hunan). Although counties and townships provide most government services, they rely on a slim tax base, collecting only 20 percent of total government revenue. In 1999, counties generated revenue barely equal to two-thirds of their spending, and about 40 percent of counties can pay for only half their expenditures.

The fiscal conditions for township governments are even more precarious because townships have practically no tax base and must extract their revenue from farmers, mostly through inefficient and coercive collection. The responsibilities of providing public services while supporting a bloated bureaucracy have forced many township governments deeply into debt. For instance, a survey in Hunan in 2000 found that township debts equaled half the province's total revenue.

In most countries, the state's declining fiscal health portends more serious maladies. The problems of the rural provinces should serve as an urgent warning to Beijing because these are historically the most unstable regions in the country, having previously generated large-scale peasant rebellions. Indeed, it is no coincidence that these agrarian provinces (where per capita income in 2000 was about half the national average) have in recent years seen the largest increase in peasant riots and tax revolts. Left to their own devices, local governments will not be able to provide effective remedies. A workable solution will require reforming the flawed fiscal system at the top and restructuring local governments at the bottom to make them more efficient and responsive.

ANGER MANAGEMENT

THE INSTITUTIONAL DECLINE of the ruling party and the weakness of the state have caused rising tensions between the state and society. The number of protests, riots, and other forms of resistance against state authorities has risen sharply. For instance, the number of collective protests grew fourfold in the 1990s, increasing from 8,700 in

1993 to a frightening 32,000 in 1999. The size and violence of such incidents have grown as well. There were 125 incidents involving more than 1,000 protesters in 1999, and the government itself admits that protests with more than 10,000 participants have become quite common. For example, in March 2002, more than 20,000 laid-off workers participated in a week-long protest in the northern city of Liaoyang. In rural areas, many towns have reported mob attacks by peasants on government buildings and even on officials themselves.

To be sure, rising social frustration results partly from the hardships produced by China's economic transition. In recent years, falling income in rural areas and growing unemployment in the cities have contributed to the rising discontent among tens of millions of peasants and workers. But the increasing frequency, scale, and intensity of collective defiance and individual resistance also reveal deep flaws in Chinese political institutions that have exacerbated the strains of transition. Social frustration is translated into political protest not merely because of economic deprivation, but because of a growing sense of political injustice. Government officials who abuse their power and perpetrate acts of petty despotism create resentment among ordinary citizens every day. These private grievances are more likely to find violent expression when the institutional mechanisms for resolving them (such as the courts, the press, and government bureaucracies) are inaccessible, unresponsive, and inadequate.

In rural China, where institutional rot is much more advanced, the tensions between the state and the peasantry have reached dangerous levels. In a startling internal report, the Ministry of Public Security admitted that "in some [rural] areas, enforcement of family-planning policy and collection of taxes would be impossible without the use of police force." In some villages, peasant resistance has grown so fierce that local officials dare not show their faces; these areas have effectively became lawless.

The most important source of this anger is the onerous tax burden levied on China's most impoverished citizens. The effective tax rate in 1996 for the agrarian sector (excluding village enterprises) was estimated at 50 percent. In fact, collecting taxes and fees has become practically the only task performed by public officials in rural areas, consuming 60–70 percent of their time. In some areas, local officials have even recruited thugs in their collection efforts; such practices have resulted in the illegal imprisonment, torture, and even deaths of peasants who are unable to pay. What has irked the peasantry even more is that their high taxes appear to have brought few government services in return. The combination of high payment, heavy-handed collection, and inadequate services has thus turned a large portion of the rural population against the state. Recent polls conducted in rural areas found that peasants consistently identify excessive taxes and fees as the most important cause of instability.

Significantly, relations between the state and society are growing more tense at a time of rising income inequality. To be sure, the reasons behind this process are extremely complex. Although the most important causes of overall inequality are the growing rural-urban income gap and regional disparities, the level of income inequality within regions and cities has been rising at an alarming pace as well. Recent surveys have found that inequality has become one of the top three concerns for the public. In the context of rampant official corruption, this rising inequality is likely to fuel public ire against the government because most people believe that only the corrupt and privileged can accumulate wealth. Such a perception is not off the mark: one academic study estimated that illegal income contributed to a 30 percent increase in inequality during the 1980s.

The absence of pressure valves within the Chinese political system will hamper the regime's ability to reduce and manage state-society tensions. Recent reforms, such as instituting village elections and improving the legal system, have proved inadequate. The CCP's failure to open up the political system and expand institutional channels for conflict resolution creates an environment in which aggrieved groups turn to collective protest to express frustrations and seek redress.

The accumulation of state-society tensions will eventually destabilize China, especially because the dynamics that generate such tensions trap the CCP in a hopeless dilemma. Rising tensions increase the risks that any reforms, even implemented as remedies, could trigger a revolution. Alexis de Tocqueville first observed this paradox: repressive regimes are most likely to be overthrown when they try to reform themselves. This sobering prospect could deter even the most progressive elements within the CCP from pursuing change.

Minxin Pei

REMEDYING CHINA'S mounting governance deficits should be the top priority of the country's new leaders. At present, these problems, brought on by the contradictions of dot communism, are serious but not life-threatening. If the new leadership addresses the institutional sources of poor governance, the CCP may be able to manage its problems without risking a political upheaval. The unfolding succession drama, however, will get in the way of meaningful change in the short term. Proposing even a moderate reform program could jeopardize a leader's political prospects. Moreover, undertaking risky reforms would require a high level of party unity—unlikely from a leadership jockeying for power.

Thus, China's governance deficits are likely to continue to grow and threaten the sustainability of its economic development. The slow-brewing crisis of governance may not cause an imminent collapse of the regime, but the accumulation of severe strains on the political system will eventually weigh down China's economic modernization as poor governance makes trade and investment more costly and more risky. The current economic dynamism may soon fade as long-term stagnation sets in.

Such a prospect raises questions about some prevailing assumptions about China. Many in the Bush administration view China's rise as both inevitable and threatening, and such thinking has motivated policy changes designed to counter this potential "strategic competitor." On the other hand, the international business community, in its enthusiasm for the Chinese market, has greatly discounted the risks embedded in the country's political system. Few appear to have seriously considered whether their basic premises about China's rise could be wrong. These assumptions should be revisited through a more realistic assessment of whether China, without restructuring its political system, can ever gain the institutional competence required to generate power and prosperity on a sustainable basis. As Beijing changes its leadership, the world needs to reexamine its long-cherished views about China, for they may be rooted in little more than wishful thinking.❷